Is Management For Me?

Copyright © 2022 by Emerge Publishing Group

All rights reserved. No part of this publication may be reproduced, distributed, or transmitted in any form or by any means, including photocopying, recording, digital scanning, or other electronic or mechanical methods, without the prior written permission of the author, except in the case of brief quotations embodied in critical reviews and certain other noncommercial uses permitted by copyright law.

ISBN (hardback): 978-17360251-0-9
ISBN (paperback): 978-17360251-1-6
ISBN (ebook): 978-1-7360251-2-3

Cover design and formatting by Albatross Book Co.
albatrossbookco.com

For permission requests, please contact: info@emergegroup.com

Is Management For Me?

For Those Who Want to Manage and for Those Who Don't!

Sheldon L. Loar
with James D. Wentworth

Contents

INTRODUCTION - Why You Need to Read This Book 1

ONE - Begin With Your Motives 9

TWO - Management Requirements 35

THREE - Leadership Expectations 53

FOUR - A New Leadership Framework 81

FIVE - Management Blindspots 119

SIX - Confessions of a Hiring Manager 146

SEVEN - Is Management for Me? 164

EIGHT - Choosing <u>Not</u> to Be a Manager 169

CONCLUSION 183

EMERGE LEADERSHIP JOURNEY 185

ACKNOWLEDGEMENTS 187

NOTES 191

*To our amazing families who shared the ups and downs
of building the business.
Without their support and encouragement, the creation
of this book would never have occurred.*

Sherry Loar	*Kelly Wentworth*
Heather, Justin, Holli, Heidi	*Katelyn, Jenna, Christina*

➤ INTRODUCTION
WHY YOU NEED TO READ THIS BOOK

"IS MANAGEMENT FOR ME?" You have likely asked yourself this question many times. Or maybe you haven't. Perhaps, you are already a manager and have been for years. Regardless, I believe *you need to read this book*.

How do I know? Let's just say I have a hunch. If any of the following descriptions fit you in any way, then I would encourage you to read on.

- ◆ You are not a manager or team leader but have wondered about the possibility of becoming one.
- ◆ You are an experienced manager with direct reports, and at least one of them has expressed interest in becoming a manager (or team leader).

- ◆ You are a senior leader who manages other managers with some downline accountability for new first-line managers.
- ◆ You have some type of responsibility for promoting, recruiting, or hiring new first-line managers.
- ◆ You are an executive who wants to create an environment where your downline leaders will start to think differently about how they prepare and select the future leadership of your organization.

The following story will help illustrate the WHY of this book and how it has the potential to save you a tremendous amount of time, money, frustration, and possibly, someone's career.

"I AM RESIGNING MY POSITION"

"What I learned today is that I don't want to be a manager! I am calling my boss tonight, and I am resigning my position."

Aiden, a new first-line supervisor at a Detroit-based auto parts manufacturer, had just spent the day with a roomful of peers. They had worked through exercises and applied tools from *The Leadership Transition*,[1] a workshop for individuals transitioning to first-line management roles.

As both co-founder of Emerge Leadership Group and the facilitator for the session, I was surprised by his comment. I thought: Wait a minute, this does not make sense! 'Quitting your job' is not on the list of learning objectives for the class!

Confused, I asked him the only question I could think of: "Why?"

Without the slightest hesitation, he answered, "I just want to be an engineer; this is what I'm good at; it's where my passion lies; it's where I want to focus my career."

As we discussed his decision, it was clear he was not doing this out of fear of the new position, nor was it a 'knee-jerk' reaction—something he decided without really processing it. I had the distinct impression this had been in the works for some time, and the training content helped provide the validation he needed to settle on his decision. His logic was sound. He had clarity of purpose. He was self-aware and had demonstrated tremendous courage by admitting that the management track was not his thing. I was impressed.

> **"Honesty is the first chapter in the book of wisdom."**
> —*Thomas Jefferson*

As our conversation ended, I wished him luck, and he turned to walk away. He seemed happier, or relieved, or maybe both.

Just as he got to the door, he stopped as if he had overlooked something. He turned around and said, "I forgot to mention that my boss will be attending your workshop here tomorrow morning." And without another word, he was gone.

My heart skipped a beat. Oh, great! Aiden's boss would be attending the *Maximizing Your Impact*$^{TM\ 2}$ workshop for leaders of leaders the next day.

I was not exactly thrilled to face an angry senior manager whose rising star had just resigned because of our course content. Ouch!

As you can imagine, I did not sleep particularly well that night.

The following morning, about 40 minutes before our session started, Aiden's boss walked into the room. We had never met, but I guessed who it was because it was unusual for anyone to be there that early. He walked directly up to me, introduced himself, and said, "I received an interesting call last night."

"Yes, I figured you probably did."

Then, something happened that I was not expecting; he smiled, extended his hand, and said, "I just wanted to thank you."

I was stunned.

He continued, "If Aiden were unhappy in this role, and continued feeling this way for a few years, eventually he would leave for an opportunity elsewhere—or if he were underperforming, we would have had to let him go.

"In either case, we would have lost twice; first, when we lost a great engineer, and second, when we lost a manager. Because we caught this early enough, I was able to put him back into his previous position. We had not backfilled it yet. Now he has returned to the team as an engineer, and everyone is happy!"

This story was unusual because most experiences like this one do not end well.

THE PROBLEM

In our decades-long experience working with thousands of new first-line managers across the globe, we have discovered nearly 65% do not meet the behavioral expectations of their roles.[3]

We have also learned that if this does not change quickly, these managers become increasingly frustrated, as do their direct reports, their bosses, and others who work with them.

This frustration can encourage them to leave the organization voluntarily, or more painfully – wait until the organization leaves them.

Here is the problem: *once you are in a management position, it is incredibly difficult to move back into an individual contributor role without some type of collateral damage.*

- For instance, you will probably have to find work at another organization if you leave your management position, and your previous role has been filled.
- A pay reduction is likely as you move from being a manager back to being an individual contributor.
- Depending upon the circumstances, you may need to physically relocate, impacting not only you, but others who may be living with you.
- There is an emotional factor to deal with as well. The human tendency to remember your failed attempt at management can take a considerable toll on your self-confidence.
- The organization may face major financial implications. According to one study, conservative replacement cost estimates were upwards of two times annual salary.[4] For example, if your income is $80,000 per year, the cost to replace you will be close to $160,000. That is not insignificant.

- There could be political ramifications for your boss or others who may have put your name forward, vouching for your potential to be a successful manager.

THE OPPORTUNITY

Deciding to move into a management role is a big deal. It is not only a career-altering experience but a life-altering one as well. Once you commit, things will never be the same.

Therefore, this book takes a preemptive approach to the self-imposed question, "Is Management for Me?" It also has a dual purpose:

- If you decide management **IS** for you, *this book will significantly increase the probability of your success by helping you prepare for the role <u>before</u> stepping into it.*
- If you decide management **IS NOT** for you, *this book will help increase the impact you can make to the organization as an individual contributor—in a profound way.*

The principles, concepts, and ideas will be helpful to those who are considering roles where they do not have direct reports but are responsible for influencing others without formal authority. So, whether you decide to pursue management or not, it will be a win for you!

A NOTE TO THE READER

For clarity, let me share some organizational features and the purposes they provide:

- ◆ **KEY POINTS:** Be on the lookout for these nuggets of wisdom specific to the chapter content covered throughout the book. Here is an example:

  > **KEY POINT:** *A primary reason for new manager dissatisfaction is misaligned expectations.*

- ◆ Toward the end of Chapters 1-6, you will find a series of questions related to that Chapter, designed to help you decide: "Is Management for Me?"
- ◆ At the very end of Chapter 1 is the beginning of a five-part Content Application Story entitled: **"A Business Dilemma: I Want to Be a Manager."** Its purpose is to help apply the content of each chapter. It concludes in Chapter 5.
- ◆ You may have noticed the compass in the bottom right-hand corner next to the page number (e.g., page 7). The spindle will move to the right at the beginning of each chapter, indicating your progress through the book.
- ◆ Lastly, you will encounter QR codes throughout the book. Scan these with your phone to find additional content specific to the topic near each code.

I use stories to help teach the concepts in this book. I have changed most of the names of the people characterized in these events to protect their privacy and any risk associated with disclosing information regarding the organizations they represent. The names of these organizations, and in a few instances, their industry, have also been changed to ensure confidentiality.
—Sheldon Loar

➤ CHAPTER ONE
BEGIN WITH YOUR MOTIVES

In the *Introduction "Why You Need to Read This Book,"* I shared the story of Aiden, a new engineering supervisor who faced a dilemma. He thought he wanted to follow the management path with its many perks. Some examples include career advancement, pay increases, status bumps, and more decision-making ability.

Then, once there, he recognized that what drove him was the need to be a world-class engineer. Aiden wisely understood how difficult it would be to maintain excellence at both. He faced a *motive conflict* and decided to slip back into his engineering role.

In this first chapter, you will try to discover your own motives, those drivers moving you to consider a potential career in management. You will also become aware of *motive trouble spots*, like Aiden experienced, helping you avoid a poor career move.

THE POWER OF MOTIVES

Several years ago, my daughter, Heidi, and her husband Ryan lived in a small college town. Ryan was trying to finish up an undergraduate degree in preparation for dental school. Even though he had a scholarship covering tuition and books, they struggled financially to make ends meet.

> "Motive: something (such as a need or desire) that causes a person to act."
> —Merriam Webster

He worked part-time at a utility management company in a customer support/maintenance role. After working for about a year, his boss approached him and asked the following question: "Ryan, have you ever considered going into management?"

Ryan had considered it but did not believe he could be a candidate because of his part-time status. His boss continued, "We have been discussing it, and we believe you would be a good fit. I am moving to a different position, and therefore my team manager role will be available. Would you be willing to apply for it?"

Ryan thought about it. This new management opening was just what he and Heidi needed. It would provide a significant increase in pay, and even though he would be required to work full-time, the opportunity was just too good to turn down. He applied for the job and received the promotion.

What was Ryan's primary motive? To satisfy the need for more income—and there is absolutely nothing wrong with that. Most of us, under the same circumstances, would do the same thing. If you think about it, there would be very few interested in taking on the demands of a management position if the reward were to make less money.

But if it were just about the money[5] (and the operative word here is 'just'), then Ryan's ability to survive the rigors of a management role would have probably faded when difficult times arrived. And they did come sooner than he expected.

Am I saying because his primary motive was money, he would have ultimately failed as a manager? No, not at all. When I asked Ryan to think back on this experience, he confirmed his top driver was the desire for more income. But as he continued to reflect, it became clear there were additional motives present, beyond a bigger paycheck. Combining these motives helped establish a foundation to give him the capacity to get through his initial difficulties in the role. What were these additional motives?

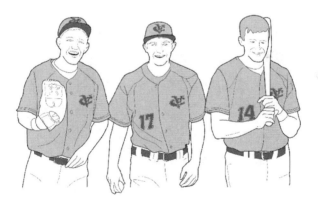

Ryan had some prior management experience; it was not much, but it proved helpful when looking for more motives. He had been an assistant manager at a restaurant, and he held multiple leadership roles while playing sports in high school.

As I spoke to him about these past experiences, he became visibly excited several times during the conversation. In sports, he not only loved the competition, but he had also come to understand and appreciate that winning took the entire team, not just one superstar. Therefore, fostering a spirit of teamwork was a high priority for him.

He also succeeded in helping certain team members improve their skills. The personal growth and development he experienced in the process helped him recognize the value of learning to coach, train and teach. Lastly, he just enjoyed being in charge.

Following high school, these motives transferred seamlessly from sports to his role as an assistant store manager at a restaurant before he headed off to college.

MOTIVE COMBINATIONS

Were all of Ryan's motives important, and did they all have value? Certainly. But they were important and valuable for different reasons. Therefore, I asked him to think back on his experience and place them into two separate categories: Primary and Secondary.

Primary Motives

These are the heavyweights – the ones that moved him to action. Remember, his main driver was more income. But as he thought about it, he identified three others he considered heavyweights: a rise in status, teamwork, and personal growth and development.

> **Ryan's Primary Motives:**
>
> ◆ Gaining an immediate income increase (to help him get through school).
> ◆ Achieving a rise in status.
> ◆ Creating a spirit of teamwork.
> ◆ Experiencing personal growth and development (transferable to his future career).

Secondary Motives

These are considered lightweights. But this does not mean they are unimportant. They still motivate and drive action, just in a different way than Primary Motives do.

For instance, one of Ryan's Secondary Motives, the fact he enjoyed being in charge, would not be strong enough to drive him to pursue a management position (neither alone nor coupled with another motive). However, this perk would help strengthen his resolve when difficult situations confronted him later.

> **Ryan's Secondary Motives:**
>
> ◆ Experiencing competition (he wanted to prove to himself and others he could do it).
> ◆ To develop coaching and training skills.
> ◆ To grow his team's capability – helping them to be successful.
> ◆ To be in charge of others.

Ryan was fortunate that he had additional motives working for him, even though I doubt he consciously thought of them as such. In our view, the most successful managers have multiple motives in both categories working in their favor. Many of these managers are aware of these motives, even though they may not fully understand the value, strength, and stability they represent in combination with one another.

The following analogy illustrates how the combined strength of two elements working together can provide a solid foundation.

BUILDING A STRONG FOUNDATION

In 2013, my wife, Sherry, and I decided to build a home in a suburb of Phoenix, Arizona, USA. Building a home was something neither of us had ever participated in, so we were excited about the opportunity. Although stressful at times, it turned out to be a positive and relatively painless experience, and we learned some interesting things along the way. One was regarding the concrete foundation slab upon which the home would be built.

> **"It is not the beauty of a building you should look at; it's the construction of the foundation that will stand the test of time."**
> —David Allen Coe

For most of my teenage years, I worked summer breaks for several residential construction companies. Each summer, a different focus. The first year concrete, then painting, followed by roofing, landscaping, and framing. Therefore, I had some knowledge regarding several processes.

Still, it had been more than 40 years, and much had changed during that time. For instance, I understood the importance of a strong foundation for any load-bearing structure—like a house. I knew the ground had to be adequately prepared, and enough rebar-reinforced concrete had to be used to withstand extreme temperature fluctuations and ground settling, which can cause concrete to split and crack. But I also knew that even with great care in preparing and pouring a foundation, there was still the possibility of it breaking and cracking over time. What I did not know was this process had improved significantly since the 1970s.

One evening, we drove by the lot to look at how things were progressing with our home. I noticed something that surprised me. The concrete crew had everything framed up in preparation for pouring the foundation. What I thought looked like rebar crisscrossing the complete footprint of the home turned out to be steel cables inside of plastic sleeves running the entire length and width of the foundation. The ends of each cable protruded outside the frame. Each one was anchored with a metal plate. The next day they poured concrete over these cables. Once the concrete had cured or hardened, tension was placed on each cable, creating compression – literally squeezing the concrete slab.

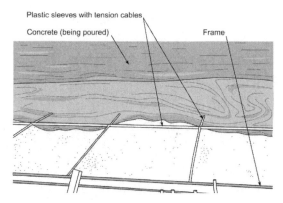

Here is the interesting part, concrete has excellent compression strength (when squeezed) but is weak in the opposite sense, which is tension (being pulled apart). Steel is strongest when it is in tension. Therefore, "putting a concrete slab into compression and the steel into tension…puts both materials into their strongest states."[6] Now, this is a compelling concept!

Ryan's primary motives are his concrete foundation. They are the principal substance—the load-bearing material, the base upon which Ryan will build his management structure. His secondary motives represent the tensioned steel cables. These cables crisscross inside his concrete foundation, anchored on all sides. And although they are not the foundation itself, they provide the tension needed to put his foundation (primary motives) into their strongest state. Conversely, the tension puts the steel cables (secondary motives) into their strongest state.

> **KEY POINT:** *Combining primary and secondary motives will help keep a manager from cracking or breaking under the intense pressure of a management role.*

Ryan experienced some of this intense pressure following his promotion. His direct reports, who were his former peers, showed initial resistance to this young, upstart college boy. After all, they were technically more experienced, and most were older than he was. The strength of his foundation allowed him to keep perspective, ultimately gaining the respect of his reports over time.

WEAK FOUNDATIONS

Tree roots growing up under a concrete sidewalk will cause it to buckle; extreme freeze/thaw temperatures can cause cracking and splitting, and salt or chemicals used to melt ice can also damage concrete.

Like tree roots, salt, and extreme temperatures, improper motives can cause your foundation to buckle or crumble when being pushed or pulled apart by outside forces. This example supports the need for Secondary Motives to help shore up and strengthen your foundation.

If motives are not accurately analyzed, you may assume you have a strong foundation, but in reality, it could be weak, causing it to crack and crumble.

The following are examples of potentially weak motives. Knowing about them and taking steps to avoid them can help you prevent or eliminate potential adverse outcomes.

WRONG OR UNCLEAR MOTIVES

For many years, we worked with a multibillion-dollar global nuclear power company. It had a robust, 16-week new manager onboarding program. It was impressive. Our role was to kick off the program to help new managers understand the critical mindset shift that had to occur to lead others effectively.[7]

There was a manager in one cohort who did not want to participate in this program. During classroom learning, he would continually check his phone, log on to his laptop, and disengage from his peers during group discussions. I found out later he was annoyed with leadership development, so he continually tried to wiggle out of commitments during the entire process.

> "A wrong motive involves defeat."
> —Mary Baker Eddy

Kristina, our contact and the program manager, was baffled by his behavior. She tried multiple times to engage him in conversation, determined to learn what was at the heart of his disengagement, especially when so many other first-line leaders in the company were begging to get into the program.

Kristina finally asked him, "Why did you go into management in the first place?" He could not come up with a reason beyond, "The position was open, and I applied for it." So maybe his motive was, "I needed a job, and this was a job."

As she dug deeper, he finally admitted, "You know, I just don't like working with people." She was stunned. Why would someone go into a role despising its most fundamental component—working with people? It would be like becoming a veterinarian when you dislike animals.

> **KEY POINT:** *Make sure your motives are clear and your rationale is solid.*

Although it seems obvious, it is surprising how many people make big decisions like this without thinking them through.

FALSE ASSUMPTIONS

A false assumption is believing something is true when it is incorrect and lacks proof of any kind, thus leading to flawed decision-making.

Hopefully, the following examples will stimulate your thinking as you seek to discover potential false assumptions you may have with your motives.

Example #1: "Increased Status should be on my list of motives because everyone wants a status increase."

Increased Status, or any other motive that sounds good can be an example of a false assumption, especially if it is the last thing driving you to consider management.

Not everyone pursues a management role for the same reasons. Stop and ask yourself: "Is this really important to me, or does it just sound good?" Doing this may help you avoid an unnecessary mistake.

> **KEY POINT:** *If a motive is unimportant to you, it has little value and will only weaken your foundation.*

Example #2: "The organization's environment will automatically support my motives."

For instance, you join an organization that encourages fairness and equality and does not value title or status. Let's assume one of your primary motives is to climb the corporate ladder as quickly as possible without consideration for others. If that is the case, this opportunity will not be the best fit for you.

KEY POINT: *Make sure your motives align with the company's vision, mission, values, and culture.*

CONFLICTING MOTIVES

Aiden (Introduction, pp. 3-5) resigned from his position because he realized he had a motive conflict. He wanted to be a world-class engineer, and he also wanted to be among the top supervisors in the company. He wisely recognized he could not do both, and the engineer motive won out in the end because it was more important to him. He did the right thing for the right reason.

As Chinese philosopher, Confucious wisely said, *"The man who chases two rabbits catches neither."*

> **Note:** Most frontline managers are working managers, meaning they must be managers, and they must also do what many of their direct reports do (e.g., be an engineer). The difference with Aiden was his desire to be a world-class engineer, to be among the best in his profession. His management responsibilities would have limited his ability to accomplish this goal.

An opposite example will prove instructive here. There is a legendary story among the consultants in our organization about Camila, a food scientist, promoted to a first-line manager, and later to a manager of managers at an international food manufacturer located in Minnesota, USA. She was highly respected by her direct reports and others in the organization as a top-rate leader.

While discussing the difficulty of making the transition from individual contributor to manager, one of the class participants raised his hand, turned to her, and asked, "How did you do it?"

Camila thought for a moment and said: *"I fell out of love with the beakers[8]."*

What a profound statement! Over time, Camila made a value shift by letting go of her passion for food science and, in its place, developed a passion for the members of her team.

Begin with Your Motives | 21

This value shift did not mean she disliked the science she was once passionate about; it simply meant that her people became more important to her than doing the technical work herself. Camila consciously chose the management path and left a legacy. She did not allow a conflict of motives to cause issues in her relationships with her team members.

KEY POINT: *You can increase the strength of your foundation by developing a genuine desire to improve the lives of the people you lead.*

Having a desire to develop people will come naturally to some, but it may be difficult for others. If this is something you struggle with, you are not alone. Many feel uncomfortable with this activity. However, keep in mind that it may not be as difficult to grow into it as you might fear.

Zora Neale Hurston summed up a great solution when she said: *"There is nothing to make you like other human beings so much as doing things for them."* Her advice is sound. You can come to appreciate and care about people as you generally try to help them be successful. This kind of approach supports the basic principle of a servant-leader, and Camila was an excellent example of someone who had adopted this mindset.

Those who cannot let go of the need to focus their effort and energy on their expertise will struggle to become high-impact leaders. Instead, they will tend to compete with their people for the best work and the glory that comes with it.

> **KEY POINT:** *Check for possible conflicts, especially as it relates to your long-term career goals.*

For example, if one of your goals is to be the CEO, and at the same time, you value having a good work/life balance with plenty of time away from work, then you may be in for a surprise. The time demands on a CEO are intense.

NEGATIVE PERCEPTIONS

Motives such as power, ambition, and money can appear unfavorable due to news reports and stories of people who misuse them. Consider the number of full-length films, TV series, and true-life crime documentaries with characters (usually bad ones) whose deeds include one or more of these three motives driving their actions.

But power, ambition, and money are neither good nor bad. It is the way they are used which determines the answer. Just as some misuse them, many others utilize them to create positive and productive outcomes.

These are formidable drivers, and there is a strong business case suggesting you need them if you want to get to the C-Suite.

> **KEY POINT:** *Do not discard a motive you feel strongly about because of negative perceptions.*

Instead, adopt a positive attitude towards it, focused on helping others, improving team results, and making a difference in the organization. If you do this, you will develop a positive reputation and will likely create productive, long-term alliances with influential people along the way.

OVERCONFIDENCE

Much has been said and written about whether people have to work to be good leaders, or are they just born that way? At Emerge, we believe in the former. To be truly outstanding, you must develop your leadership capability. It takes work, persistence, patience, and time.

However, we recognize that people have abilities they were born with or characteristics that come naturally to them, which could lend themselves to succeeding in management and leadership.

We conducted many interviews in preparation for writing this book. One of the questions we asked was: "What motivated you to go into management?" There were many different reasons, as you might imagine.

However, on occasion, we would interview someone who responded like David, a long-time friend, and client.

When we asked him this question, he paused for a moment, looking a bit puzzled. Then he said, "You know, as I think back as far as I can, back to when I was a kid, I have always tried to lead; I had a passion for it.

I never wanted to be the quiet one in the room. I wanted others to hear and consider my opinion, from Boy Scouts to playing football with my friends. When the opportunity came, I tried to be the one to help lead the team. I liked being the one out front."

David clearly had natural characteristics driving him to manage and lead, but they did not automatically make him good at it; they just helped him along the way. They made it easier for him as he was naturally more confident in those settings.

For example, David assumed that people would just do what he asked them to, "I'm the boss, now follow me."

He continued, "I was aggressive in my early management years and had to learn to listen, have empathy, and encourage others. I had to recognize that it was not about me. It was about members of the team and the team itself."

Learning these lessons and developing the associated skills—working in concert with his natural abilities has helped him become the invaluable leader he is today.

> **KEY POINT:** *Having a management title does not automatically make you a leader. You must earn the trust and loyalty of those assigned to work with you.*

THE ROLE OF DISCIPLINE

To ensure your motives deliver their full potential, consider the part *discipline* plays in the equation.

Clinical psychologist Jennifer Johnston-Jones, Ph.D., stated: "When you hear [the word] 'discipline' do you think 'punishment?' Most people do...the meaning has been altered from its original form. The true meaning of discipline is 'to learn' or 'to teach' which came from the Latin *disciplina*."[9]

Most of us can relate to the Latin definition, especially with the word "*learn*." You probably would not be reading this book if you had not experienced some level of success in your life as a result of discipline.

Motives provide the initial spark causing you to act, and they remind you why you are doing what you are doing. When you get off track—they help you get back on track, going in the right direction.

Discipline fans the flame, helping it grow into a fire as you focus on the task at hand. Ultimately, you will begin to see results. As positive outcomes start to surface, you will more than likely stay on course and improve your ability to manage and lead, making it easier and more rewarding. The gift of discipline is the formation of a behavior into a habit. And developing good habits is the hallmark of success.

> "Habits stay with you even when you don't have the motivation."
> — *Neeraj Agnihotri*

COMMON MOTIVES

At the beginning of the Emerge learning experience on this topic, we ask participants to share their reasons (motives) for signing up for the class and considering a management role.

The following list constitutes the most common motives or reasons they share with us. As you look through the list, ask yourself about the strength of each one. Is it solid enough for either a Primary or a Secondary motive? Would it help someone survive the rigors of the role?

- "It is the next logical step in my career."
- "I enjoy challenging people to stretch and grow."
- "I'm ambitious. Status is important to me. I want to be a CEO someday."
- "I've been here a long time and feel that I deserve the position."
- "Others have helped me be successful in my career. I want to *pay it forward*."
- "The financial rewards are really attractive to me."
- "I'm the best on the team – it just seems to make sense."
- "I feel like I could utilize my organizational skills in an expanded way."
- "There's nowhere else to go in the organization – management is the only option."
- "I would like to travel more. A management position would give me that opportunity."
- "I find it rewarding to coach and develop others."
- "I love process improvement – to make things better for the team and organization."
- "I'm bored with my current position – I need a new challenge."
- "Being involved in helping to determine the direction of a team is exciting to me."
- "My boss keeps pushing me. She thinks I would be good at it."
- "I want to be the one in charge – to make the decisions."

- "I feel I can better help the organization grow if I'm in a management role."

BUILD YOUR MOTIVES LIST

It's time to start building your own motives list. We recommend you take the following steps:

- Write down everything that comes to mind. You are brainstorming, so don't analyze or categorize (Primary or Secondary); just let the ideas flow.
- Once you finish the brainstormed list, then analyze it. Here are some questions to help you with this step.
  - Are there any wrong or unclear motives on my list? (pp. 18-19)
  - Are there any false assumptions? (pp. 19-20)
  - Do I have any conflicting motives? (pp. 20-23)
  - Did I leave any off because of negative perceptions? (pp. 23-24)
  - Am I overconfident in any area? If yes, in what ways? (pp. 24-25)
- Next, separate your analyzed list into Primary and Secondary categories, using the following questions to guide your decisions:
  - Would this item be strong enough to drive me to make a decision? If it would, then it should be a primary motive.
  - If it would not push me to decide by itself, what

28 | Is Management For Me?

if I paired it with another motive (name each item on your list)? Would the combination of the two change my mind? If it would, it is likely an additional primary motive.
- If the item is not strong enough to drive a decision (either alone or paired), it should be a secondary motive.

> **Note:** Remember, your *Primary Motives represent the concrete*. Therefore, they need to be substantial enough to cause you to take action. I cannot tell you what substantial should look like. Everyone is different, so you must decide.

The *Secondary Motives* represent the tension cables. They are not the foundation, they support and strengthen the foundation – they make it better.

CONTENT APPLICATION STORY

A Classic Business Dilemma

More than a decade ago, I met with a group of vice presidents from a financial services software company in Manhattan, New York, USA. The topic of discussion was how to strategically improve the identification, selection, and preparation of individual contributors for first-line leader positions.

I will never forget the look of dismay on the face of

one executive as he shared with the group a dilemma he was facing. One of his top salespeople had decided she wanted to be a manager and threatened to leave the organization with her multi-million dollar book of business if she did not get her way.

A competitor understood this and was trying to recruit her by offering her a management position in their company. The executive said, "If I promote her, she will be a terrible manager! But if I don't, she walks out with a significant portion of my revenue plan. It will hurt us in a big way! I feel caught between a rock and a hard place."

He was right! He *was* caught between a rock and a hard place. I do not know what decision he ultimately made, but I am assuming he caved to the pressure, opting to keep his revenue in-house, and instead tried to work around her management inadequacies.

She might have become an outstanding manager if he kept her by promoting her, although I think it is improbable based on his assessment.

In most situations like this, the company, the manager's boss, and those reporting to the manager all suffer as they live with an ineffective manager.

We have heard this same story repeated many times through the years, with the only changes being the names of the people involved and their unique circumstances. For this reason, we will use an example in the form of a narrative to help apply the content from Chapters 1-5.

The title of this narrative is *Content Application Story: "I Want to Be a Manager!"*

Part 1 will begin here, in Chapter 1. The story will continue with Parts 2-4 at the end of those chapters, and the Conclusion will be in Chapter 5.

The primary objective of this story is to help you, the one considering a career in management, find insight, perspective, and in some cases, even validation as you try to discover your answer to the question: *"Is Management for Me?"*

CONTENT APPLICATION STORY: THE BEGINNING

"I Want to Be a Manager!" (Part 1)

Jacob, an operations research analyst for a mid-sized insurance company, sat across the desk from his boss, Adeline. "I'm ready for my next assignment," he said. "I want to be a manager."

Adeline was surprised – but at the same time – not surprised. Jacob was ambitious, articulate, and incredibly bright. He received an undergraduate degree in math from a respected university, followed by a master's degree in physics from another university.

Jacob was a great college recruit and quickly became a top-rate analyst, becoming one of the best on Adeline's team. He had worked in her department for nearly two years and had become highly respected by his colleagues for his technical abilities.

But becoming a manager this early in his career? Adeline felt it was premature – doable but risky. She decided to dig a little deeper to discover his motives for pursuing management.

"Why are you so interested in management?" Adeline asked. "You seemed to be thriving in your analyst role. Everyone talks about how good you are."

Jacob smiled and shifted in his chair. "I do like what I am doing, but to be candid with you, I need a *new challenge*." He paused for a moment and then continued, "I feel like I've learned about all I can in this role, and I want to keep growing. I'm ready for something different."

"Does anything else attract you about a management role?" Adeline asked.

"Well, I like the idea of a *pay raise*.

I also feel I could *help others be better at their jobs*. And I guess the *increased respect* I would get from the new title intrigues me as well," he concluded.

"How would you categorize these?" Adeline asked. She explained the concepts of Primary and Secondary motives to him.

"What is this, some kind of test?" Jacob asked.

"Well, sort of." She responded. "I like to see what is driving someone's decision. Often, there are other ways to fill the need rather than always defaulting to the promotion solution."

"For example, if you were to say your only reason for moving into management was a *new challenge*, then I would most likely look for some other way of helping you."

"Makes sense," Jacob said. He then categorized the items and put them in order of priority.

Adeline was encouraged that he had four motives. They were certainly good enough to get him started, but she knew, depending on the person, *New Challenge* and *Pay Increase* could equate to, "I want a new challenge and another pay increase" a year from now if he became bored again.

Jacob's Primary Motives:

Primary:
- New Challenge
- Pay Raise

Secondary:
- Increased Respect
- Help Others.

Based on her observation of Jacob and her previous experience with other professionals who had been in similar circumstances, she simply did not feel Jacob was ready. He needed more time and more seasoning. It was too soon.

She knew he would not like her answer.

"Jacob, I like your ambition. I believe you are headed in the right direction and will make a great manager, but I believe you are not quite ready for this kind of experience yet."

"Why not?" Jacob demanded. "I'm the most qualified – I am the top performer on the team! I'm ready for this if you will give me a chance!"

"I do not disagree with most of what you have said, Jacob. You are a real asset to this team and the organization. I just want to make sure you have a successful experience, and I think it will happen with a little more time."

There was a short but tense pause. Then Adeline said, "I have an idea. Why don't I work on crafting a development opportunity for you? A project that will give you a sense of what it's like to be in this type of position. You can try it out, see how you like it, and I can observe and see how well you do? Then we can reevaluate at its conclusion."

Jacob liked the idea. Adeline would need some time to put a plan together, and then they would coordinate a meeting to discuss the project details and get Jacob moving.

(To be continued in the next chapter)

> **CHAPTER TWO**

MANAGEMENT REQUIREMENTS

ROLE RESPONSIBILITIES

Every role in every organization has specific responsibilities or requirements to complete as part of the job. Many of these are not negotiable; they are vital components of the role. It is crucial to be aware of them. The following example illustrates what can happen if you are not.

Rita was a successful retail technology salesperson who worked for an internationally recognized and highly respected computer manufacturer. With an outgoing personality and an ability to connect with people, she was a natural.

She had a good manager who cared about her development and gave Rita opportunities to train other salespeople, an activity she found incredibly rewarding. Because she enjoyed this so much, she pushed for a sales manager position, and after some time, Rita received the promotion she wanted.

She told me, "I was excited about the prospect of working more closely with my salespeople. I thought I would be spending most of my time doing this. But shortly after the promotion, I was reminded of the other role requirements, like overseeing processes, attending meetings, producing a series of weekly reports, and managing scheduling."

With more than a hint of sarcasm, she said, "My absolute favorite, without question, was scheduling! I had to make sure the floor was covered every moment the store was open. I had to coordinate holidays and vacations, manage sick leave, and deal with no-shows. It took up a crazy amount of time! I told my boss this wasn't part of the deal! I thought I was supposed to be helping my team get better, be more productive, and sell more."

She continued, "I told him I spent more time with them when I was one of them than I did now as their manager. And to me, this just did not make sense!"

Rita ended up frustrated and disillusioned because so much of what she was required to do was administrative. Ultimately, she quit the sales manager position and left the organization.

MISALIGNED EXPECTATIONS

In our experience working with thousands of managers across the globe, we have found many stories like Rita's. These managers were doing some of

> "It's a lack of clarity that creates chaos and frustration."
> —Steve Maraboli

what they expected they would do, but there were additional requirements they were either unaware of, ignored, or did not take seriously.

> **KEY POINT:** *A primary reason for new manager dissatisfaction is misaligned expectations.*

Misaligned Expectation Examples

The following illustrations may help you avoid falling into similar traps if you determine that management is for you.

> **Observation:** *Managers who have a pre-established set of expectations and are unwilling to adjust them when the role's requirements turn out to be different.*

This was Rita's issue. We should all understand that perfect alignment can happen but is not typical. A little flexibility on your end will show others your willingness to evolve and embrace change – a highly sought-after behavior. Also, recognize, remember, and be thankful for the occasional experience that exceeds your expectations. You encounter them, perhaps more than you realize. It shows maturity on your part to remember and appreciate this fact.

> **KEY POINT:** *Be receptive to the possibility that you may need to adjust your expectations for the role you are considering.*

Observation: *Managers who focus on what they want and skip over the unappealing role requirements.*

I would suppose we have all been guilty of this at one point or another. Let's say you want a new car in a big way. You try to justify it by becoming hyper-focused on the many reasons you should do it. You look at the list of advantages and benefits, and interestingly, you downplay, minimize, and outright ignore some of the disadvantages (e.g., the cost). Then later, you agonize over the poor decision you made and ask yourself, "What was I thinking?

KEY POINT: *Do not skip the fine print. Ensure you understand each requirement and its implications before committing to a promotion.*

Observation: *Managers who are aware of the role requirements and are willing to accept them. But they do not have the skillset to complete them.*

In this scenario, they are simply unprepared. But knowing about the role requirements makes this a favorable situation. Why? You are not walking in blind.

KEY POINT: *Training, coaching, and time will typically resolve a skills disparity issue if you are at least aware of them and are willing to learn what is required.*

Observation: *Managers who are entirely unaware of specific requirements. They simply do not know what they do not know.*

In our experience, this is the most challenging group and the main culprit of misaligned expectations. Helping you avoid this issue is of primary importance and thus a vital goal of this chapter.

KEY POINT: *Identify the hidden management requirements for the role before accepting it.*

UNDERSTANDING THE WHAT AND THE HOW

From this point forward, we will refer to *management requirements as <u>what</u> needs to be done*, those specific responsibilities that define the role. These include the day-to-day transactional work responsibilities establishing the purpose of the position—the reason the role exists in the business.

Good managers know their jobs well, understand <u>what</u> they need to do, and execute effectively on those specific items.

The focus of this chapter: *Management Requirements*, will be to identify the requirements of the role you are considering: to figure out <u>what</u> must be accomplished and become clear on the many responsibilities you will have as a manager.

In the following two chapters: (*Leadership Expectations* and *A New Leadership Framework)*, I will introduce you to a model designed to improve <u>how</u> you can complete the requirements of your role in a more powerful way.

BECOMING <u>AWARE</u> AND BEING <u>WILLING</u>

Simply stated, you must be *<u>aware</u>* of the requirements of your role, and you must be *<u>willing</u>* to change to meet those requirements. Although this might sound obvious, remember the story of Rita, an example of a talented professional with good leadership capability and a promising future. She was not *<u>aware</u>* of the time it would take to meet the other requirements of her role. Rita's singular focus was developing her sales team, to the exclusion of many other responsibilities. Once she realized how much time the other requirements were taking, she was un*<u>willing</u>* to accept the required changes and opted out instead.

As we consider Rita's situation, we could make the case that this issue was not entirely her fault. After all, she "didn't know what she didn't know." Does this mean her manager shared some of the blame for this? Probably. But in the end, Rita had to own this. It was her responsibility to understand the requirements of the role that she had accepted.

To help you avoid the mistake Rita made, you should become *<u>aware</u>* of the management requirements of the role you are considering and strive to understand the purpose of each one.

You can document these requirements and use this information to decide if you are *<u>willing</u>* to make necessary changes to meet the expected outcomes they are supposed to produce.

KEY POINT: *Everything is changing at breakneck speed. Your <u>awareness</u> of these changes and your <u>willingness</u> to learn and adjust will be crucial to your career success.*

As you do so, others will recognize you as a high-performance manager, one who will not fall victim to misaligned expectations, the cause of so many frustrated new managers.

YOU DON'T KNOW WHAT YOU DON'T KNOW

Think about the management role you are considering. Can you define the requirements of the position? I am confident you would give a good description of everything you have *personally observed*.

But there is a problem with this. Your vision is limited or restricted. Like peering out of a window, you only see what is inside the window frame. Your limited vision constitutes your reality with the role.

Anything outside the frame, beyond your sight, represents additional management requirements you cannot see, leaving you in a precarious situation because *you don't know what you don't know.* You are vulnerable as you sign up for something that may potentially blindside you.

I remember early in my career, joking with my peers as we imagined what our manager did when he was not working directly with us. He was a great boss, but our interactions with him were limited by what we observed him doing through our window. Because he was not with us all the time, we assumed he was perhaps out playing golf, having lunch with his buddies, or sleeping. Of course, none of us sincerely believed this, but the point is, we simply did not know (and technically, we did not need to know).

Since then, I have learned about some of what he did "outside" of our view – things we were not aware of at the time. I discovered he was under a lot of pressure from corporate and upper management. He worked extremely hard and did much more for us than we assumed.

For instance, he did a masterful job acting as a type of firewall, filtering out the noise and corporate flack constantly exploding all around us. Anything he felt would be an unnecessary distraction—something that would divert our attention or keep us from getting our work done – he tried to eliminate, which was no small task.

THE UNWRITTEN AND UNSPOKEN ORDER OF THINGS

An essential part of the work you will do in this chapter will be to identify or uncover the unwritten and (or) unspoken order of things in the organization where the position is located.

What do I mean by the unwritten and unspoken order of things? These are the requirements neither in an employee handbook nor in a job description. They vary, not only from organization to organization but from role to role.

For example, let us hypothetically say that an office equipment and supply company headquartered in Australia has two offices: one in Sydney, New South Wales, and the other in Melbourne, Victoria. They are approximately 900km apart.

Both locations are identical in their branding and in the products and services they offer. They are also remarkably similar in how their various functions operate. You would assume that the same management roles in each location would be nearly identical. To be more specific, you could imagine the credit manager roles in both locations to be essentially the same from a management requirements standpoint.

Yet, there are several differences. For one, the credit manager in Melbourne has tremendous freedom and flexibility to make her own hiring decisions.

The Sydney office is different. Leadership in this location limits the involvement of the credit manager. Instead, they have opted for a more tightly controlled hiring process, including recruiting and interviewing teams, predetermined interview questions, and specific selection criteria.

As a final example, I will share an experience while consulting at a mid-sized manufacturing organization in Pennsylvania, USA. I had the opportunity to talk with Ricardo, a recently hired fabrication assembly supervisor.

The company was operating 7-days per week, 24-hours per day, running three shifts. They employed supervisors to cover each shift.

Ricardo told me, "When I originally applied for the night shift supervisor position, I was under the assumption that all fabrication assembly supervisors had the same job descriptions and responsibilities – based upon the information they gave me for the job.

"However, after accepting the position, I discovered that because production slowed down at night, the night supervisors did not have as many staff to manage. And because of this fact, the night shift supervisors had no administrative help – a benefit the day shift and swing shift supervisors enjoyed.

"This left most of the administrative tasks for me to handle personally." He shook his head slowly and then glanced over his shoulder.

"Look, I get it. I have fewer employees to manage, so I should be able to handle some of this stuff. But still, it would have been nice to know before showing up for work the first night? I didn't realize I had signed up to be my own administrative assistant."

Not being aware of this undocumented fact was frustrating to Ricardo. He said, "Someone should have told me!" And he was right; they should have. But there are always going to be nuances like this in every organization.

An informed decision will require additional research to understand what the role entails. You can often find job descriptions, including role requirements, on job posting sites like LinkedIn, CareerBuilder, Monster, and many others. The company's website or the Human Resources department can provide valuable information as well.

The data you gather from those sources will be invaluable. *But remember, what you are looking for are the unwritten, unpublished requirements* – the stuff that can blindside you.

The best information source is the person who currently occupies the position or someone who had the job in the past.

Imagine the difference it would have made for Ricardo

to have a conversation with a former night shift supervisor who revealed the additional responsibilities he would have to shoulder. Would he have still taken the job? I tend to think so, but he would have had a much better attitude during those first few weeks.

Consider having similar discussions with other first-line managers or supervisors in the organization, even though they may be in different departments or functions. Patterns may emerge, expanding the size and scope of your window frame. The more you understand the organization's management requirements, the better.

Hopefully, this will play to your advantage as others see you taking the initiative to understand the role you are considering.

KEY POINT: *Pay special attention to the unwritten and unspoken requirements. These are not generally in the job description or employee handbook.*

BUILD YOUR MANAGEMENT REQUIREMENTS LIST

To begin building your list, apply the window frame analogy to the management role you are thinking about and answer the following questions:

- ◆ What do I know about the management requirements for the role I am considering – those I can see through my window?

- What do I ***not*** know about the management requirements, beyond the window frame, outside my view?
    - Remember, *you don't know what you don't know.* Asking this question will likely stir up your memory, which should help you recall some things you may have observed but forgotten.
    - Consider discussing this topic with your colleagues, supervisor, and others, asking for their experiences, perspectives, and insights.
- Is there someone you could talk with to find out more information on the role requirements?
- Try to arrange an interview with someone currently in or who has occupied the role in the past. If this is not possible, find someone who at least knows the role well. If you can schedule some interviews, consider asking the following questions:
    - "Once you were in the role, what surprised you or caught you off guard?"
    - "What parts of the role did you find particularly difficult to master?"
    - "What elements of the company cultural were you unfamiliar with?"
    - "What did you like most about the role?"
    - "What did you find least rewarding about it?"
    - "What coaching, tips, or suggestions would you give to someone new to this role?"

The following table contains a sample management

requirements list. Its purpose is to help you create a customized list of your own. Do not assume all of these items should be on your list. Every management role is unique and will have its own set of requirements.

Most of the items on this list could be written or unwritten requirements depending upon the organization.

SAMPLE MANAGEMENT REQUIREMENTS LIST

- Oversee the operations of a team
- Increase productivity
- Keep staff engaged
- Provide vendor management
- Maintain morale
- Encourage teamwork
- Deliver team results
- Oversee supply management
- Forecast and budget
- Provide career development planning
- Delegate responsibility
- Hold others accountable for results
- Deal with challenging personalities
- Hold performance reviews
- Provide balanced feedback
- Resolve conflict
- Give necessary disciplinary action
- Document processes
- Produce reports
- Coach team members
- Provide training

- Deliver new employee onboarding
- Drive continuous improvement
- Oversee time-off approvals
- Track and manage schedules
- Connect team goals to organizational goals
- Manage time
- Be a liaison between staff and management
- Manage change
- Run meetings
- Present results to higher-level management
- Maintain technical/functional competence
- Work on team building
- Provide program development
- Meet with clients
- Free up team from unnecessary tasks
- Remove obstacles
- Coordinate with sponsors
- Select and hire talent
- Let people go (fire)
- Encourage robust discussion
- Communicate up
- Provide recognition and rewards
- Determine team priorities

You may have noticed that many of the items on this sample list are not specific enough. For example, *Run meetings*. Running a meeting does not tell you anything about it. If this were one of your management requirements, it would be helpful to know: the name, objective, frequency, and the attendees for each meeting.

I should mention here that it is easy to get caught up in analysis paralysis or perfectionistic thinking. As you assemble your list, understand that it is probably not realistic to discover every possible requirement or detail.

Any information you can gather that will give you a sense of the position and what it entails (including the *unwritten and (or) unspoken requirements*) will put you miles ahead of others who may be vying for the same position and not even thinking about this issue.

And we are just getting warmed up. Other tips and ideas like this will help give you a leg up on the competition. By completing this book, you will have a strategic advantage over others competing for the same role.

CONTENT APPLICATION STORY

"I Want to Be a Manager!" (Part 2)

Part 1 Review

We continue the story we began at the end of Chapter 1 regarding Jacob and Adeline. If you recall, Jacob, an operations research analyst, pushed his boss for a management position. He was certain he was ready for it. His boss, Adeline, was certain he was not.

To provide him with some experience, she committed to construct a development assignment – a project for him to work on to see how he would do.

Part 2 - Continuation

After their initial meeting, Adeline went to work on creating a project for Jacob. She was taking this seriously. Jacob was a great employee who had a promising future, and she did not want to lose him.

Once Adeline had the development plan ready to present to Jacob, they sat down and worked through the details.

The project included an opportunity to lead a high-value project with a cross-functional team assigned to him. This project had the potential of providing good visibility and exposure for Jacob. If it went well, critical people within the organization would recognize his potential.

He would need to work with some key stakeholders, communicating progress throughout the life of the project.

One of the more challenging aspects of this assignment would be motivating his team members to complete the project on time. Each team member had a different direct-line manager, and each of those managers had a list of priorities that Jacob's team members would need to work on at the same time.

Finally, as part of the deal, he would also be required to complete his regular duties – a daunting task.

Jacob was excited about the new opportunity. He threw himself into the work and learned quickly. Adeline did her best to observe him, receiving permission from the managers of his team to get feedback from them occasionally.

She was impressed by his determination. She

noticed he spent a tremendous amount of time on this assignment, knowing he still had to complete his regular duties. It was stretching him in a big way.

Jacob was able to focus and complete the work at an intense pace. He was a quick learner and became adept at each process and management requirement.

Jacob had assumed those who indirectly reported to him (his team members) would complete their assigned tasks. He fully expected them to own these tasks and assignments; this was just how things were supposed to work.

It caught him completely off guard when he realized how difficult it was to motivate people to meet his expectations. He could not wrap his head around how cavalier some of them seemed about their responsibilities. When they did  complete them, it was barely on time and, in some cases, late, which impacted other aspects of the project and other teams depending upon them to finish their assigned portion on time.

This issue became a huge hurdle for Jacob. Of course, he knew each team member reported to a formal manager, meaning—he was not their boss. However, for some reason, he did not process this fact thoroughly. Those managers had different priorities which they expected their direct reports (his team members) to complete. When it came down to what got done, his work was always second in line. He ended up in several confrontations with members of the team over this issue.

Maintaining quality expectations was another challenge. It was vital to Jacob. His name was on the line with this project. The outcomes they produced had to be as perfect as possible and completed the way he thought they should be completed.

Unfortunately, not everyone was as meticulous with the details or shared the same vision as he did. A few of his team members would quickly handle the items they were responsible for, not paying attention to the quality Jacob required, prompting him to do or redo much of the work himself.

When the project was complete and delivered to the client, Jacob was exhausted but satisfied with the results. It was refreshing to him, and he genuinely enjoyed the experience. He and Adeline scheduled a project review at its conclusion.

(To be continued in the next chapter)

➤ CHAPTER THREE
LEADERSHIP EXPECTATIONS

REQUIREMENTS VERSUS EXPECTATIONS

The focus of the last chapter was *Management Requirements* – the non-negotiables, the stuff that defines the role. It was about <u>what</u> must be done as part of the job.

The focus of this chapter is *Leadership Expectations*. It is about <u>how</u> people assume you will accomplish those requirements.

> **"The quality of our expectations determines the quality of our action."**
> —*Jean-Baptiste André Godin*

When you receive a promotion to any formal or informal management role, an interesting phenomenon occurs. As a new manager, you will have a set of leadership expectations imposed upon you.

In the context of our discussion, requirements are different from expectations. Expectations are not mandated. Let me give you an example. Let's say you expect your manager to communicate project outcomes with you effectively. He communicates them, but he does so in an ineffective, confusing way. What happens? Probably nothing. You recognize that he is a poor communicator and must tolerate him until he leaves. We can *expect* him to behave a certain way, but we cannot mandate or *require* him to do so.

> **Note:** Some organizations have leadership behaviors that are part of a manager's key performance indicators – a fantastic idea! You would think every organization would implement this, but it is not as common a practice as you might assume.

KEY POINT: *Your ability to recognize and adjust your behavior to meet these leadership expectations will ultimately determine your success as a leader.*

AWARE AND WILLING (REVISITED)

We continue the topic of "Aware and Willing" from the previous chapter (Management Requirements). Similarly, you must become aware of the Leadership Expectations that others have of you an*d be willing to make the behavioral modifications to meet them.*

Understanding and embracing this principle will give you a significant advantage over those who are unfamiliar with it.

Let's say that, yesterday, you were a confident, productive technical superstar. But today, you receive a promotion. Now, you are the manager, and a dramatic change has taken place. It is uncomfortable and unfamiliar, causing you to feel way out of your depth. Why? Expectations change the moment the promotion is announced, making it difficult for you to adjust – especially if you are unprepared. How do you prepare? By making a transition.

AN INTRODUCTION TO TRANSITIONS

Let me introduce you to the remarkable concept of *Transitions*. You are likely familiar with this word, but how we use and apply it is unique.

> **KEY POINT:** *A transition begins as you become aware of new expectations that others have of you and willingly adjust your behavior accordingly.*

There are five different transitions you can make during the span of your career. I will refer to each set of expectations as a *Stage*. The expectations differ from one Stage to the next and contain adjustments in several essential areas, including:

- ◆ Acquiring different kinds of work skills.
- ◆ Increasing the number and types of relationships you have.
- ◆ Broadening and lengthening your time perspective.
- ◆ Making a mindset shift – changing the way you think at the new Stage.
- ◆ Expanding/changing the kinds of work you value.

For example, suppose you are an individual contributor and determine you want to be a manager. In this case, you must make a transition from meeting the behavioral expectations of a high-performing technical/functional expert to meeting the behavioral expectations of a highly effective leader. These expectations are entirely different. You must change from a self-focused mindset and approach to one that seeks to help others, enable the team, and ultimately impact the organization.

> **Note:** There are several transitions required of individuals throughout their careers. These will be discussed in greater detail during the next chapter "A New Leadership Framework."

TRANSITIONS AND TIME

A critical component of a successful transition is time. There are two specific facets of time within the context of a transition:

- First, the amount of time spent at each Stage, and
- Second, the amount of time it takes to transition from one Stage to the next.

The time requirement in both cases may vary dramatically, either alone or when combined with other factors, including:

- Role complexity: The more complex the role, the more time required.
- The specific Stage: Some Stages require more time than others.

◆ The person making the transition: Depending upon the expectations of the Stage, some individuals are more motivated and (or) have a natural knack to move faster than others.

CREATING MOMENTUM

Our culture has evolved dramatically since the advent of the Internet. Before it existed, it was challenging to get the information that you needed. You had to attend college, spend time at the local library, purchase newspapers and periodicals, and mail letters requesting specific information; all of this effort to gather a small fraction of what you can access on your smartphone in seconds today. According to one source, Google handles 3.5 billion searches per day.[10]

In the workplace, we are given projects and assignments, and if there is something we don't know how to do, we search until we find out. This environment has trained us to become "want-it-gotta-have-it-now" consumers. We are accustomed to, although not always comfortable with, lots of rapid change. It is crucial to career survival to anticipate and adapt to change quickly. If we do not, we will be left behind.

Yet when it comes to transitions, patience plays a crucial role. *A transition cannot be forced or rushed.* Behavioral change does not occur overnight.

KEY POINT: *A transition occurs when those around you begin to trust you as you show capability and gain credibility. They are the ones who determine when you transition.*

You may be familiar with the famous Marshmallow Experiment conducted by Walter Mischel, a Stanford professor, on a bunch of 4 and 5-year-old children back in the 1960s.

With cameras rolling, a child was brought into a private room, they were seated in a chair, and a marshmallow was put in front of them.

Before leaving the room, the researcher would tell the child they could eat the marshmallow now, or if they waited and did not eat it until the researcher returned 15 minutes later, they would be given a second marshmallow.

Many could not resist and ate their marshmallow within a few moments. A few managed to wait the entire time and were rewarded with a second treat.

I do not believe anyone was overly surprised by the results. I wondered what I would have done had I been part of this experiment. I'm not a big fan of marshmallows, so I certainly would have been grouped with those who waited, but, alas, for the wrong reason.

The fascinating part of the story came with the follow-up study conducted years later. The researchers made an amazing discovery. Those willing to wait patiently – to delay gratification – had higher SAT scores, better responses to stress, better social skills, and were overall more successful in life.[11] [12]

There is a message in this that applies to the pursuit of a management role. Let's assume you are not quite ready, and there is no management role available for you to apply for anyway. What do you do? *We advocate patience. Not the passive, sitting around, quietly waiting for a position to become available, kind of patience. Rather, the persistent, deliberate, action-oriented kind.*

> **KEY POINT:** *Active patience is the type where you prepare, improve, and train — but wait for the right opportunity to come along.*

Active patience helps create transition momentum. How?

- By intentionally learning and practicing new skills
- Deliberately growing your network
- Where possible, making yourself visible to others
- Finding a coach or a mentor to give you essential feedback

This approach is much better than just waiting for the phone to ring or an email to arrive with a management offer.

Someone said, "Good things come to those who wait." I would change this quote to say, "*Better things come to those who actively wait.*"

I was fortunate to have a mentor at a young age—someone who took a genuine interest in me and my development. David[13] was my mother's younger brother, and even though he was years older than I was, we had (and still have) much in common. He has remained a significant influence in my life to this day.

During a difficult time in my career, David counseled me to be patient but not standstill. He would say, "Keep your feet moving, *but be careful not to try to force things to happen.*" He suggested that I take deliberate action with a calm (rather than frantic) sense of urgency, allowing things to unfold as I went along. "Things will often turn out better than you might expect," he said. This counsel has proved true on many occasions. It is what I mean by *active patience.* The future manager who understands this concept will have a much higher likelihood of success.

TRANSITION EXAMPLES

A transition in our terminology means (in most cases) letting go of certain behaviors that have helped you be successful in one Stage and embracing new ones to help you be successful in the next Stage.

To help illustrate the importance of these transitions, I will present examples of three different managers at various points along the transition continuum.

- ◆ The first manager has not begun the transition.
- ◆ The second manager is in the middle of her transition.
- ◆ And the third manager has fully transitioned.

As you read through these examples, note the impact each has on others relative to where they are in their transition.

A Non-Transitioned Leader

In the marketing department of a large health services organization, Sophie, a content writer, shared an experience with me about her boss, the internal communications manager, whom I will call Nia.

Sophie told me, "The culture in our company is pretty relaxed. A lot of autonomy is given to each division, allowing it to do whatever it wants to acquire and purchase support services like recruiting, custodial, equipment maintenance, etc.

"Because these internal services were not equipped to sell their value, they were slowly being eroded by external vendors."

Sophie continued, "Management gave our team the assignment to create a marketing strategy to help recapture some of the business that had been contracted out. The objective was to raise awareness and show the value and benefits of utilizing the company's internal capabilities.

"Nia called a meeting with me and her other two direct reports to collaborate on a plan. When we met, we began to make suggestions and share ideas, but it became apparent that Nia had already decided on a solution as she politely turned down each idea not aligned with hers. We got the impression we were simply playing a guessing game until we arrived at the conclusion she had already determined.

"We later discovered that Nia, in her excitement, had worked nights and weekends to develop a strategy and had everything planned out, down to the finest detail, including an impressive presentation to be pitched to each division's leadership team.

"It was disheartening to the three of us (Nia's direct reports) to be left out of the idea creation and plan development parts of the process. But we still recognized the value it represented, and we were impressed with Nia's creativity, so we jumped on board to support it."

Sophie paused for a moment and then said, "It gets worse. When the division marketing managers learned about the plan, they were also supportive and were excited to be involved. We saw an opportunity to build bridges and develop allies by partnering with the division marketing people, but Nia would not have it. She only trusted her team to make the presentations and oversee the implementation. In her mind, there was too much at stake. If this went well, it would give us (mostly her) a lot of credibility." Sophie said.

She concluded, "Of course, the division managers were annoyed at Nia's inflexibility and unwillingness to let them participate."

Even though Nia completed *what* she was asked to do (create a marketing strategy to recapture lost business), she missed several significant opportunities because of *how* she approached and completed them. Nia's team and the division marketing managers assumed they would be involved in the process. They expected Nia to partner with them, help them learn something new, and contribute to the project's success. She was completely *unaware* of these expectations.

Her vision was self-focused, and she struggled to let go of control and trust her direct reports and other capable professionals to help contribute to a winning project. In the end, the project did not produce the results it had the potential to deliver. Nia lost credibility with many in the company, which was the polar opposite of her expectation.

Even though she was a "get-it-done" professional with

an eye for quality, Nia had not begun to make the transition from individual contributor to leader. She, therefore, was not prepared to step into a management role when she did. She had been promoted too early.

A Transitioning Leader

In this example, Olivia, a clothing store manager, has begun demonstrating a different mindset. Although she is somewhere in the middle of her transition, she experiences an improved outcome because her perspective has changed.

Olivia had been in the retail clothing business her entire career. She was dependable, knowledgeable, and experienced—she knew her stuff! Because of this, Olivia was promoted to store manager and learned the requirements of the role quickly.

About a year later, she was approached by a competing store in a neighboring city with an attractive offer to fill one of its store manager roles. She accepted the offer.

As Olivia was settling into her new surroundings, one of the management requirements she was responsible for caught her off guard. The task itself was nothing new to her as she had a similar responsibility in her prior role.

Olivia was required to produce a detailed *sales forecast and store profitability* report. This report was generated monthly and was utilized by senior management to help make critical business decisions.

Producing this report constituted *what* needed to be done – a *management requirement* of the written kind. It was in the job description, and Olivia understood it clearly. But what she did not understand was *how* the report was expected to be produced, a *leadership expectation* of the unwritten kind.

Instead of producing the report herself, as she did at her previous job, it was assumed Olivia would meet *the leadership expectation of utilizing her staff to produce this report.*

Because she was *unaware* of this expectation, she did it herself, causing some team members to feel she did not trust them. Olivia sensing something was amiss, pulled her team together to talk about it. Olivia listened, asked questions, and committed to letting them handle this process in the future.

She then went to her boss to try to understand the purpose behind it. Her boss explained that the team members felt more trusted, needed, and respected by sharing this responsibility. It helped broaden their perspective – allowing them to see how their work aligned with the organizational strategy and positively (or negatively) impacted its goals. And lastly, there was a noticeable increase in pride and ownership of the employees' work.

Her boss made it clear to Olivia that she expected her to look for other opportunities to provide meaningful development experiences like this—to think and act more strategically in her approach to her work.

Olivia was emotionally mature enough not to become defensive about the feedback. After all, no one had explained this process to her; she only found out about it after she had completed it. Olivia learned from this experience and worked to understand and internalize the value of such an approach.

Her *willingness* and commitment to be more sensitive and *aware* of this new organization's leadership expectations suggest she's making the transition. As she adjusts her approach, the contribution she makes will positively impact her people and the business.

A Transitioned Leader

As a final example, I share the story of Theresa, a former client and current Emerge Leadership Group consultant.

Early in Theresa's career, she worked at a well-respected, fast-paced technology company. She was a competent individual contributor who worked hard at her craft and consistently demonstrated her ability to be aware of what was happening around her. She picked up on cues occurring over the process of time that were related to changing expectations others had of her as she matured in her profession.

Theresa practiced active patience. She was innovative, helped develop others, understood her team's vital role in the organization's success, and communicated that vision to everyone around her. She was constantly curious, asking questions and challenging the status quo.

Theresa was fortunate to have a good manager who saw her potential, not as a threat but as an asset to the team and the organization. She provided Theresa with opportunities to lead while she was an individual contributor. *When the team leader position became available, Theresa was the obvious choice to everyone on the team. No pushback. No power struggle.*

Theresa was allowed to show her capability and credibility as a leader long before the promotion happened, making the process seamless.

GOOD MANAGER – BAD MANAGER

Since 2008, the kick-off activity for our Leader of Others[14] and Leader of Leaders[15] learning events is an exercise we call: "Good Manager – Bad Manager."

This activity works to help illustrate how leadership effectiveness has a direct impact on business outcomes. Participants identify the ineffective behaviors followed by the effective behaviors of managers they have worked with during their careers.

We have assembled a combined list from one of the classes we taught in Europe several years ago (see the following table).

Leaders who consistently mirror behaviors similar to those on the left will negatively impact business outcomes like employee engagement, customer satisfaction, employee turnover, and company profitability. Those leaders whose behaviors are more in line with those on the right positively impact those same business outcomes.

Ineffective Manager Behaviors	Effective Manager Behaviors
• Unwillingness to prioritize • Not transparent • Micromanager • Does not trust • Poor communicator • Will not hold others accountable • Unapproachable • Does not provide balanced feedback • Lacks vision • Lacks confidence/insecure • Does not show empathy • Arrogant • Plays favorites • Gives unclear expectations • Physically and (or) emotionally unavailable • Refuses or struggles to delegate • Disorganized • Emotional • Overly controlling • Will not share information • Avoids conflict • Has a personal agenda	• Communicates vision • Flexible • Collaborative • Empowering • Credible • Change agent • Humble • Good listener • Caring/Empathetic • Trusting • Passionate • Authentic • Engaged • Develops – stretches • Available • Strategic-minded • Good teacher/coach • Calm under pressure • Practices what they preach • Optimistic • Gives credit to others • Takes ownership of failures

What does this have to do with our discussion on the topics of Leadership Expectations and Transitions?

First, we intuitively expect those who occupy management positions to apply the characteristics and behaviors of those in the column on the right. When they do, we recognize them as successfully making the transition (or transitioned).

Second, when they do not meet the expectations, when their behavior looks more like the left column, we sit up and notice! We recognize them as non-transitioned leaders.

I find it fascinating how individuals who have good leaders do not always recognize or fully appreciate them as much as they should. Yet they sure recognize when they are being led by a poor one!

Notice the Effective Behaviors in the right column. They most often are of the *unwritten* and even *unspoken* kind. They are not in an employee handbook, and they are not typically discussed in a job interview. Nevertheless, they are there, and they are expected.

For instance, don't you expect your manager to empower you to make decisions about your job and trust you to deliver the results you have committed to deliver? Don't you expect your manager to listen and be engaged in what you and your peers do? Of course! Yet, interestingly, those items are primarily unwritten and unspoken.

Many people would say, "This is just common sense. These expectations go without saying." And they would be right. They do go without saying (*unwritten* and *unspoken*). You will be expected to behave in these positive ways if you decide to become a manager.

Another observation: One of the people I interviewed for this book told me he had learned more about leadership from the worst manager he ever worked for than he did from his best managers. I was curious about this comment and asked him to say more about it. He said, "The way this manager treated me was so terrible, it burned an image into my brain I will never forget. It motivated me to be a better leader. It was a powerful lesson."[16]

For proof of this fact, review the Ineffective Manager Behaviors, in the table on page 68. Imagine having a boss who consistently behaved in those ways. You would never forget this person or the lessons you learned of how _not to manage or lead_.

PREMATURE PROMOTIONS

"Timmy had only two pennies in his pocket when he approached the farmer and pointed to a tomato hanging lusciously from a vine.

"Give you two cents for it," the boy offered.

"That kind brings a nickel," the farmer told him.

"This one?" Timmy asked, pointing to a smaller, greener, and less tempting specimen. The farmer nodded agreement. "OK," said Timmy, and sealed the deal by placing his two pennies in the farmer's hand. "I'll pick it up in about a week."[17]

One common reason many new first-line managers do not meet these leadership expectations is they are not ready. They need to season a little longer. Before the promotion, they were focused on meeting the expectations of a high-performing technical/functional professional in an individual contributor role and were likely doing a marvelous job. *But then the promotion happened, and expectations changed immediately.*

You need to think like Timmy in the story above. Apply it to yourself. Are you ready? Or are you still too green? If you decide to be a manager, start working on the transition now, so you'll be prepared to be "pick[ed] up in about a week," or, more realistically, a year.

Succession Planning

Most organizations focus succession planning at the senior and executive levels of the organization, which makes complete sense. Leaders are groomed for years, taking on different roles, provided with stretch assignments, training courses, and personal coaching.

But *the frontline level –* where the work happens, *is largely left unattended regarding succession planning.* We observe that most organizations *wait until a promotion occurs and then scramble to help these new managers transition before doing too much damage.* And for this, we at Emerge Leadership Group will be forever thankful, for this has been and continues to be the work we do, the value we provide for our clients. When a group of new managers is ready or assembled, they call us, and we come running in to help these new managers navigate the most challenging transition they will most likely experience in their entire careers.

But let us get back to the issue at hand. There is a tremendous risk associated with this kind of approach. The average time required for a new leader to make the transition settles in at somewhere between *three to five years if they try to do it on their own—and this is for the few who successfully make it.

This is an enormous amount of time for someone to figure out how to be effective on the fly as they attempt to manage and lead those who do the actual work—the ones who interact with the organization's or internal team's customers.

Consider the implications of this, and pair it with the following statistic. *"Companies fail to choose the candidate with the right talent for the job 82% of the time."*[18] If this is happening, then employees and customers are both being negatively impacted. We believe there is a much better approach.

KEY POINT: *Begin developing individual contributors earlier. Give them opportunities to grow leadership capability now rather than waiting until they are in a management position.*

How does this apply to you, the one reading this book, the one trying to decide if the management track is right for you? Hopefully, the message has been loud and clear: *"start making the transition now!"* It is much easier to navigate it as an individual contributor versus a new manager who has all the expectations heaped upon them all at once and, in most cases, is ill-prepared to handle them. The sooner you start, the better.

> ***Note:** Given the right tools and a direct manager who has also transitioned and who is committed to hold new frontline managers accountable for leadership work, the transition can be shortened to less than a year.

FEEDBACK

Soliciting and receiving feedback may be one of the most underutilized development opportunities on the planet. Why? Because people are generally afraid to give or receive what is called *constructive feedback*. They don't like to feel they are being judged or criticized. For example, those providing feedback can experience defensiveness, making it an unpleasant experience for them.

It's so much easier to give and receive the happy kind. It makes everyone feel great, but its value is limited at best. The not-so-happy kind (*constructive)* is where the helpful information lives, the type that will provide you with the most value.

Do some self-reflection. How are you at encouraging people to give you feedback? Do you make it safe for them? Do you show gratitude and implement the (appropriate) recommendations they provide?

Decide now to make regular feedback a tool to learn what leadership expectations others assume you will adapt to, and don't wait until your annual review to find out. Seek it out often. You'll be amazed at what you discover.

KEY POINT: *Soliciting and receiving feedback may be one of the most underutilized development opportunities on the planet. Learn to give and receive it regularly. It will help accelerate your growth.*

In Chapter 7 – Is Management for Me? You will do what we call a *Reality Check* – a process to help you determine if you are ready for management.

If you scan this QR Code with your phone, you can access a free online assessment. You can share it with those inside and outside of your work environment. The feedback they provide can be invaluable as you work to make a decision.

CONSIDER YOUR LEADERSHIP EXPECTATIONS

Ask yourself the following questions for the role you are considering:

- ◆ What will I be expected to do from a leadership standpoint? (Examples: coach, hold team members accountable for results, handle difficult conversations.)
- ◆ **Note:** check with your Learning and Development or Human Resources department to see if they have developed specific competencies for the role you are considering.
- ◆ In what ways will I need to change or evolve in the following areas?
    - ▸ Work skills? (e.g., from technical/functional skills to leadership skills.)
    - ▸ Relationships? (e.g., from primarily peer connections to meaningful relationships with influential people throughout the business.)
    - ▸ Time perspective? (e.g., from a few months to many months or even years.)
    - ▸ Work values? (e.g., from valuing technical/functional competence to valuing contribution and impact on people, processes, and the business.)

- Am I or my manager pushing for me to take a management position? If yes, do I sense it could be premature? If yes, how could I plan for and practice active patience? In what ways could I be preparing now?

> "If you align expectations with reality, you will never be disappointed."
> —Terrell Owens

- Review the Effective/Ineffective Manager Behaviors list and ask yourself these questions:
  - If I were a manager right now, with which ineffective behaviors would I struggle?
  - What effective behaviors would I need to develop?
  - Are there effective behaviors in which I excel? What can I do to build upon these strengths?

CONTENT APPLICATION STORY

"I Want to Be a Manager!" (Part 3)

Part 2 Review

When we last left this story, Jacob had just completed his stretch assignment where he played the role of project leader. It was incredibly challenging, but Jacob felt he accomplished what he set out to achieve. He is preparing to meet with his boss, Adeline, for the project review.

Part 3 Continuation

Adeline and Jacob met in her office at the project's conclusion. "Well, how did you feel about this development experience, Jacob?" Adeline asked.

"Great! I finished on time, and the stakeholders were happy. I enjoyed the experience and learned a LOT! There was so much to take in! But I believe it was a success." Jacob said with a look of satisfaction.

"I must admit, I was amazed by the amount of energy you poured into this project, Jacob. More than anyone I have ever seen before! I could tell you were serious about this."

Jacob beamed.

"And I was not at all surprised by how quickly you figured out the procedural and technical aspects of the project, as you have a knack for getting in and mastering those details."

"Well, I must say I had to work a lot of extra hours to get there! Fortunately, it was interesting to me. Doing most of the work myself turned out ok in the end as I learned so many great things about the project itself," Jacob said proudly.

"I did notice you put in a lot of time on this. Do you say you did most of the work yourself? Were you not getting enough help from your team?" Adeline asked.

"I was more than a little frustrated with several of the team members who did not give me the support I needed," Jacob said.

"I would assign something to them, and they would put it off until the deadline was almost here. Rather than take the risk of it not getting completed, I would jump in and just try to figure it out on my own – and in most cases, I did." Jacob looked more pleased than frustrated.

"They always had all of these other priorities from their direct managers they were working on, so it seemed like my stuff would constantly end up falling to the bottom of the priority list."

Adeline had observed this. She knew it was real, and she assumed it would happen. She had even warned Jacob about this before the start of the project. This was of primary interest to her to see how he would handle this kind of complex situation. She had to resist the urge to jump in and try to save him on several occasions. She knew the importance of failure and the experience it brought. Failure could be a good teacher.

Before the project kick-off, Adeline received approval from the managers of Jacob's team members to occasionally check in with each of them to see how things were going. Not surprisingly, she received a slightly different story from his team than the story Jacob was telling her. She knew this did not make Jacob dishonest, but rather someone with a distinct perspective, giving him a different experience.

When she met with his team members individually, each of them seemed to genuinely like Jacob. They thought he was a great person. They all thought he was amazingly smart. Yet most had become irritated with him, primarily because they felt he disapproved of their work, even though they believed it was good quality. Further, he didn't trust them to deliver what they promised to provide. Nearly everyone felt he was constantly micromanaging them.

Also, when he assumed they would not complete their assignments on time, he would jump in and do it himself without communicating anything to them, making a few of them angry. But most of the other team members did not mind at all—they learned to procrastinate, knowing he would end up doing it for them. What was to dislike about this deal?

Another annoying behavior was how Jacob would keep the high-profile, visible assignments for himself, passing the stuff no one else wanted to do – to them.

"What about the stakeholders?" Adeline asked. "How were they to work with?"

"Oh, they were the best! I tried not to bother them with too many details because I recognized they were so busy. I knew they were mostly interested in the successful completion of the project deliverables, so I did not interact with them much."

Jacob continued, "Our main goal was to deliver a quality product – on time, and we did. We met their expectations, and they were happy. This project was a win for us."

Adeline had also visited with the key stakeholders.

They said they liked him. He seemed self-assured and articulate. But they rarely saw or heard from him. Most of them were not bothered by this, as the highest priority to them, to Jacob's point, were the results. And he had delivered them. Jacob was right; they were happy.

However, what concerned Adeline most about this was Jacob's missed opportunity to connect and communicate regularly with these important people. These relationships could play a critical part in his future as a leader if he eventually moved into management.

"Jacob, you did meet the deadline and delivered a quality product on time. I applaud you for this. However,"

Jacob broke in before Adeline could continue, "So I am ready then? I knew I could do this!"

Adeline jumped back in, "Jacob, there were some outcomes I wanted to observe you doing during this experience, and I did not see them." She shared the feedback from his team members and the stakeholders.

Jacob was not happy. He spent the next several minutes defending himself, attempting to shift the blame to others, including a veiled insinuation that Adeline had set him up for failure.

Adeline patiently listened. She let him vent. The fact was, she could hardly blame him. He nearly worked himself to death and delivered a finished product – one he considered a complete success – and then she stepped in and *rained all over his parade*, telling him he missed the mark.

"I guess I just don't understand what I did wrong," Jacob finally said.

Adeline thought for a moment. "This is difficult for me to describe. But what I was looking for, above and beyond a finished product, was to see you lead.

"I know you have the technical know-how to figure everything out and do it on your own. But I needed to see you build essential relationships with your team members and with the stakeholders.

"I needed to see you working with the individual members of your team, using your influence to help them figure out how to get your priorities and their other priorities completed.

"I needed to see you resist the temptation to micromanage the details, but instead, learn to trust your people and hold them accountable for delivering on their commitments. Those were the outcomes I was looking for."

She could tell Jacob understood the words and phrases coming out of her mouth but still did not grasp what needed to change.

Adeline had to help paint a picture for him, one that would allow him to see and understand what she and the others working with him expected – beyond the finished product.

"Jacob, if you are game, I will find some additional work opportunities for you. We can keep working on this together. You have the potential to figure this out and become a good leader, and I am committed to helping you get there. I will also find a visual representation of what I am trying to say about this leadership thing I'm struggling to articulate."

Jacob was still upset but visibly relaxed following Adeline's suggestion.

"Ok, I'm good to keep at it," Jacob said.

Adeline smiled. "I'm going to need some time to work on this. I'll be in touch with you once I put something together for you to consider."

(To be continued in the next chapter)

➤ CHAPTER FOUR
A NEW LEADERSHIP FRAMEWORK

THE EMERGE STAGES OF IMPACT™

I was sharing our Stages of Impact Framework with one of our marketing vendors who needed to understand what made our company unique.

About midway through the presentation, he suddenly jumped up out of his chair, and pointing to my computer screen, cried out, "So, this is what they were trying to tell me!"

His outburst nearly scared me to death. "What are you talking about?" I asked.

"That Stages thing you're showing me! My boss, where I used to work, told me I did not have what it took to be a manager. When he said that, it infuriated me! I asked him what he meant, what I 'did not have?' But he could not give me a clear answer. He tried, but to me, it seemed like a bunch of excuses. I figured he just didn't like me."

He paused for a moment and then continued, "But this Stages Framework, as you've been describing it—makes sense to me. I believe this is what he was trying to tell me!"

This chapter is focused entirely on the Emerge Stages of Impact™ Framework. *This tool will help you make sense of the Leadership Expectations discussed in the previous chapter.*

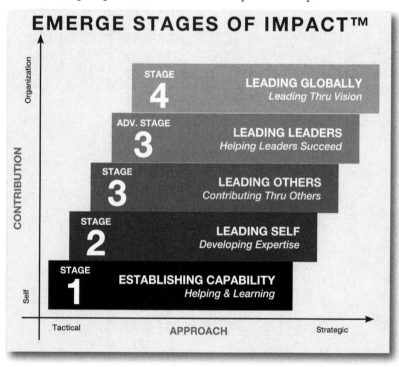

EMERGE STAGES OF IMPACT™ FRAMEWORK

The Stages of Impact Framework contains five different Stages. Each Stage has:

◆ A title (e.g., Leading Self).
◆ A number assigned to that Stage.
◆ A list of five bullet points describing its characteristics (we refer to these characteristics as the Key Accountabilities of that particular Stage).

TRANSITIONS ON HYPERDRIVE

You will recognize the oft-used word hyperdrive if you have ever read or watched science fiction films (e.g., *Star Wars*). Typical situation: the hero (and crew) are in the crosshairs of the villain who is about to blow their ship into a million pieces. Just as the bad guy pulls the trigger, the hyperdrive kicks in, and our hero's spaceship lurches forward, stars streaming in white horizontal lines as they jump into hyperspace and disappear, just in the nick of time.

The word hyperdrive is "an invented word used by science fiction writers to describe anything that can power a spacecraft faster than the speed of light."[19]

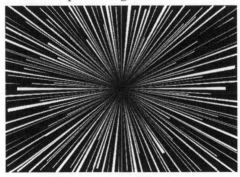

When properly understood and applied, the Stages of Impact Framework has the potential to provide a mechanism like a hyperdrive, allowing the acceleration of a transition to happen much faster than it would otherwise.

You should find this Framework and movement through the Stages descriptive of the experience you have personally had so far in your career. Therefore, we do not refer to it as a theoretical model (how we think things should be) but rather as a descriptive model (how things really are).

Since transitions are so fundamental to your success, we will discuss them in detail.

Our first step is to walk through the basic components or elements of the Stages of Impact Framework. This model is simple and intuitive. There are several essential concepts or elements that you need to understand.

ELEMENTS 1 AND 2: CONTRIBUTION AND APPROACH

Two crucial elements of this framework are Contribution and Approach.

The vertical axis of the Framework is called *Contribution*. It spans from a *Self*-focused mindset at the origin and moves up to an *Organization*-focused mindset at the peak.

The horizontal axis is called *Approach*, and it spans from *Tactical* at the origin to *Strategic* at its endpoint.

There have been many great combinations in history—combining two ideas to create a synergistic event. These combinations create something new and innovative, more meaningful as a pair than separately.

> *"Synergy: the interaction of elements that when combined produce a total effect that is greater than the sum of the individual elements, contributions, etc."*[20]

A great combination was hatched in the mind of Henry Ford. He "was inspired by the meat-packing houses of Chicago and a grain mill conveyor belt he had seen. If he brought the work to the workers, they spent less time moving about."[21]

Ford applied that concept to the Model T inside his automobile manufacturing plant, and the assembly line was born. No longer did a mechanic have to work on one vehicle, perform a piece of the overall project, pick up a toolbox and equipment and walk to the next one. The assembly line changed the automobile industry forever, making vehicles more available and more affordable.

Ford assembly line (1913)

Contribution and Approach combine to help you maximize the impact you make on the organization throughout your career.

Not only does it improve the team and organization, but it also directly affects you. It does this by demonstrating to others the value you bring regardless of your position, whether executive, middle manager, front-line manager, team leader, or individual contributor.

Element 1: Contribution

Contribution is about how you think, feel, and ultimately what kinds of work you value. The way you think, feel, and value[22] must evolve or change as you move from one State to the next. This mindset shift can occur independent of your title, so even if you are an individual contributor, you can begin to shift your thinking to be more "others oriented" over time.

But you say, "Now wait a minute! I'm a package delivery driver. I'm running around, alone, delivering boxes of stuff all day long—and I'm working my tail off! How am I supposed to be thinking about helping others be successful at what they need to accomplish when I can barely get my work done? That makes no sense. It would be easy if I were in a management role and had direct reports; then, I would be working to help my team be successful as part of my job. But this individual contributor thing? I don't get it."

The question is valid, and I will attempt to answer it with an example coming up later in this chapter. To prepare, let us reexamine the Stages of Impact Framework and concentrate on the vertical axis.

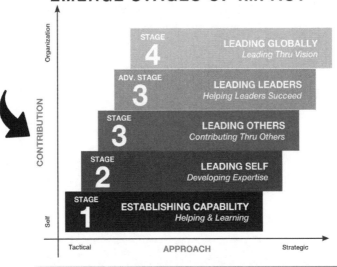

As you can see, this is where it is positioned, with a *Self-focused contribution* at the origin and an *Organization-focused contribution* at the tip. (Note: Organization is *others* oriented – the opposite of *self*).

> **KEY POINT:** *Your contribution focus must align with the expectations that others and the organization have of you.*

For example, someone within the first year of their career should have a *Self-focused contribution*. We don't want these new employees worrying about the profit and loss statement, inventory, or whether our project will meet the deadline. We expect them to focus on their small portion of the work in their small part of the company. As they develop more capability, which in most cases is rapid, they can begin to be concerned about other things, but for now, it is all about them – and this is what we want and expect of them.

Conversely, suppose you are in a management position or an individual contributor with eight or more years of experience. In these cases, the expectations others have of you will be much more *Organization* or others-focused, where you worry less about *what's in it for me* and much more about *what's in it for the greater good of others*, the team, and ultimately, the organization.

At this point, I need to make an important distinction.

Often there is confusion between the definitions of Performance and Contribution. They can be considered the same or similar. However, they are fundamentally different in the context of how we use them. Here are some definitions to help provide clarity:

> ***Performance*** = the execution or accomplishment of work.
> ***Contribution*** = how someone impacts others in the process of executing or accomplishing work.

Because contribution is defined by how you impact others as you execute your work, you have the potential of making a negative or positive contribution on others based upon your behavior.

An illustration should prove valuable at this point.

I had the opportunity to observe and work with two remarkable salespeople in the packaging, printing, and publishing distribution business.

Everyone in the entire business unit recognized both as high performers. They had consistently met or exceeded their sales objectives. Both were valuable assets to the company!

Now, here is where the concept of contribution comes into play. As we define it, contribution considers the effect these two salespeople had on others as they met their performance expectations.

Brent was intense, a great person, but relentless in ensuring his customers received the right products at the right time. He worked hard at his craft, worked long hours, and expected others to do the same.

He demanded perfection, and when someone made a mistake (every company and individual makes them), he would throw a fit – not an immature-childlike fit. But he had the reputation when something went wrong, and he came storming through the front door; people went running for the exits.

Brent achieved his numbers and reached legendary status in the company, but he did so, often at the expense of others. Support staff did his bidding more out of fear than desire. He was well-respected but not well-liked.

Hudson was different. He was calm under pressure and expected the same customer service Brent did, but he dealt with it differently. He was determined to meet his numbers, but he *built up others* rather than reprimanding those directly involved in a mistake. Hudson recognized the long-term benefit of helping people become better.

Hudson tried to develop relationships, not only in his division but across the organization. Building relationships takes time, patience, and persistence, and it paid off for him in the long run.

People were motivated to help him because of the appreciation and gratitude they received in return.

Others appreciated and recognized Hudson for the collaborative way he impacted processes that were not working well. He understood that mistakes, especially repeated ones, often result from a process problem, not a people problem.

There are incentives like trips to exotic destinations or big bonuses for top salespeople who produce the best numbers in many sales-focused businesses. This kind of environment is essential because good salespeople thrive on competition, driving the numbers up. Competitiveness with these personality types is mostly a good thing.

But the flip side of the coin is the reality that it can pit salespeople against one another. Using a salesperson example is what makes this so relevant.

Hudson understood the value of *contribution* and addressed questions such as:

- "How can I help other members of my sales team be successful?"
- "What about those in support functions who help us meet our quotas? Is there anything I can do to make our interactions less complicated?"
- "What do we do as a sales team to frustrate or waste the time of those who help us deliver value to our customers?"

Hudson was an outstanding individual sales producer who understood the value of support staff, management, and other salespeople to his long-term success—he worked to make everyone better. As a result, he made a more significant contribution to the overall organization.

> **KEY POINT:** *A salesperson, accountant, programmer, or package delivery person who understands the value of contribution and recognizes the benefit of helping grow the entire team, will ultimately be more productive in the long run.*

Often, the influence of just one person who makes this shift can help a team be more cohesive, engaged, and mindful about efficiency in solving problems by working together – rather than against one another. Along with other benefits, this shift should build better brand recognition and service quality for those customers who utilize their products and services.

> **Note:** Remember, these two salespeople were not managers; they were individual contributors. Neither of them ever wanted to be, nor were managers during their entire careers. I will address this more in *Chapter 8 – Choosing Not to Be a Manager*. The point is that individual contributors can transition to Stage 3 and make an immense impact on an organization without ever moving into management.

As we prepare to move our discussion from *Contribution* to the next element in our Great Combination – that of *Approach*, I end with a scene from the motion picture, *The Emperor's Club.*[23]

In the film, Arthur Hundert is an inspiring Classics history professor who has devoted his life to teaching at an elite prep school for boys.

It is the first day of Hundert's Western Civilization class. As the class begins, Hundert asks one of the boys, Martin Blythe, to walk to the back of the room and read a plaque hanging high on a wall above the door. Blythe reads:

> "I am Shutruk-Nahunte, King of Anshand and Susa, Sovereign of the land of Elam. I destroyed Sippar, took the stele of Niran-Sin, and brought it back to Elam, where I erected it as an offering to my god, Inshushinak."
>
> — Shutruk Nahunte, 1158 B.C."

Hundert then asks the class if anyone is familiar with Nahunte (no response).

"Texts are permissible," he states as the boys frantically flip through their textbooks.

"But," Hundert says, "you won't find it there."

Hundert strides over to a rolled-up map hanging on the wall and yanks down on a dangling string, exposing its geography.

Tapping on a specific location, he says, "Shutruk-Nahunte, King, sovereign of the land of Elam. Destroyer of Sippar."

"Behold, his accomplishments cannot be found in any history book!"

"Why? *Because great ambition and conquest without contribution is without significance.*"[24]

What a powerful statement. It is worth repeating:

KEY POINT: *"Great ambition and conquest without contribution is without significance."*[25]

In our salesperson example, Brent focuses on himself, with little or no regard for those who work with him and, ironically, on whom he depends for his success. His contribution will, in a sense, be without significance and will ultimately be forgotten. Compare that to Hudson, who understands the value of contribution and his impact on others. Hudson's legacy is the difference he made in the day-to-day lives of those who were privileged to work with him.

Element 2: Approach

We now move from *Contribution* to *Approach*. I cannot begin to express the importance of this concept.

KEY POINT: *Approach considers the "ideas or actions intended to deal with a problem, [opportunity] or situation."*[26] *The approach you take to your work influences the contribution you make.*

The illustration above shows *Approach* positioned at the horizontal axis of the Stages of Impact Framework. It moves from a *Tactical-focus* at the origin to a *Strategic-focus* at the endpoint.

Like contribution, a *strategic approach is not better than a tactical approach*. Why? Because they are connected to the expectations we have of one another.

For example, an employee, new in their career, is expected to take a tactical approach to their day-to-day work. In contrast, an experienced CEO is expected to take a highly strategic approach to their work.

The word approach and its use are intuitive, but a typical example might provide additional meaning.

In aviation, approach is one of several phases of flight. It refers to adjusting the aircraft's heading, speed, and altitude to line up as it subsequently descends toward a landing place. Therefore, *"A good landing is the result of a good approach."*

The phases of a flight include:

1. Pre-departure
2. Clearance to Taxi
3. Take-off
4. Initial climb
5. Climb to cruise altitude
6. Cruise altitude
7. Descent
8. Approach
9. Landing
10. Taxi to the terminal
11. Postflight

The U. S. Federal Aviation Administration (FAA) claims that "Over 45 percent of all general aviation accidents occur during the approach and landing phases."[27] This statistic is significant. Those two phases constitute nearly half of all accidents. And if you think about it, a certain percentage of the accidents that occur during the landing phase possibly could have been avoided with a different or better approach plan. This reinforces the critical nature of paying close attention to the entire approach process in the workplace.

Casualness in preparing for an effective approach can have dire consequences whether you are attempting to land a plane or, in our case, a crucial leadership conversation.

ELEMENT 3: TRANSITIONS AND TIME (REVISITED)

We discussed Transitions and Time in the last chapter, but they are worth a revisit here.

Some may incorrectly assume that the individual attempting to transition from one Stage to the next decides when the transition happens. This assumption has validity because the determining factor in a transition is behavior change consistent with the new Stage's Key Accountabilities. However, here is the caveat: *the people who work with you make this determination.*

How does this happen? As you successfully work to change your behavior to align with the expectations of the new Stage, those who interact with you begin to see you differently and treat you differently. They place more trust in you as they see the results you consistently deliver. They recognize your ability to do the job and meet the expectations indicated by the Key Accountabilities of the Stage. You now have *credibility*, and those around you begin to treat you accordingly.

Capability, credibility, and time are all factors in every transition from one Stage to the next. But time will vary according to the Stage, the complexity of the role, and the person.

ELEMENT 4: TITLE INDEPENDENCE

The name of the Stage may suggest an organizational title. For example, *Advanced Stage 3 Leading Leaders* sounds like it is for those who manage other managers. But each Stage is independent. It is not connected to a title. Although the expectation may be there, meeting those expectations depends upon your behavior.

A more common example would be a first-line supervisor. Because of the title, this person is expected to think and act according to the definition of *Stage 3 – Leading Others*, and yet their behavior might mirror the definition of *Stage 2 – Leading Self.*

The opposite of this is true as well. An individual contributor may develop to the point where *Approach* and *Contribution* are more clearly aligned with the Key Accountabilities of Stage 3 even without a formal title or direct reports. Someone can develop the capability and earn the credibility to be recognized as Stage 3, which, you will discover, is an enormous strategic advantage for both the individual contributor and their team.

ELEMENT 5: CHANGE REQUIREMENTS

As you might assume, a transition from one Stage to the next is not automatic. As we have discussed, a transition happens as you become aware of the new Stage and willingly adjust your *Approach* and *Contribution* accordingly. The changes require you to embrace the Key Accountabilities of the next Stage and include adjustments in several important areas, as discussed in the previous chapter, including:

- ◆ Acquiring different kinds of work skills
- ◆ Expanding the number and types of relationships you have
- ◆ Broadening and lengthening your time perspective
- ◆ Adding and (or) evolving the work you value
- ◆ Making a mindset shift—changing the way you think at the new Stage

ELEMENT 6: NO SKIPPING STAGES

It is essential to understand that a Stage may not be skipped. Success at taking a Stage 1 approach and making a Stage 1 contribution is required before moving to Stage 2 and so forth. You must develop your skill level in the Key Accountabilities. When others observe this over time, you earn credibility, and they recognize your transition.

ELEMENT 7: GETTING STUCK

It is common for most people to transition from Stage 1 to Stage 2 without significant trouble. It is a different story moving from Stage 2 to Stage 3. It is during this transition where most people tend to run aground. Getting stuck can happen for several reasons, some of which will be familiar to you. The following is a partial list:

- The person lacks awareness of the expectations of the new Stage.
- Although the person may be aware of the leadership expectations of the new Stage, they are unwilling to change their behavior to align with these expectations.
- The person may or may not be aware of the expectations of the new Stage but struggles to let go of the desire to micromanage and control the work the team is responsible for every step of the way.
- They have a passion or love for doing the work themselves, so they struggle to let others be as involved as they should be.

STAGE DESCRIPTIONS

The next step in this process will be to walk through the Stages of Impact. I will describe each Stage along with its associated Key Accountabilities.

STAGE 1 – ESTABLISHING CAPABILITY

The Key Accountabilities of Stage 1 include:

- Willingly accept direction and supervision
- Learn basic tasks
- Work on smaller tasks that are part of larger work
- Demonstrate future potential
- Exercise directed creativity and initiative

Those new to the organization or new to their career are expected to take a Stage 1 approach. Their contribution expectation is focused on "*Self.*" Therefore, they must learn how they fit into the new environment and culture. They need to get to know the people, understand the processes, and get up-to-speed as quickly as possible.

They are expected to take a *tactical* approach by helping and learning. They should ask lots of questions, absorb as much as possible, and apply their previous experience to the new environment.

If they are new to their career, there is not a lot expected of them initially. They establish capability by taking on small pieces of work. They are given larger pieces as they complete that work, ultimately gaining the credibility to transition to Stage 2 – Leading Self.

This transition for most people is intuitive and relatively short. But be careful! The temptation to rush through Stage 1 can be detrimental to one's career. The time spent doing well with a Stage 1 approach and contribution forms a strong foundation for future success and credibility.

The average time spent at Stage 1 is just six to nine months. But this is highly dependent upon the complexity of the role. The more complex the role, the longer it will take someone to transition.

STAGE 2 – LEADING SELF

EMERGE STAGES OF IMPACT™

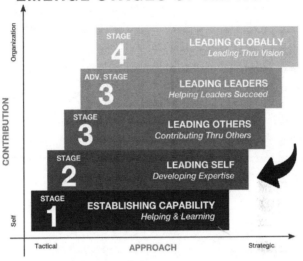

The Key Accountabilities of Stage 2 include:

◆ Plan own work
◆ Demonstrate technical expertise
◆ Demonstrate professional capability
◆ Accept and work within the organization's culture
◆ Meet professional standards for area of expertise

Stage 2 constitutes the bulk of the workforce population and the organization's backbone. It is at this Stage where the work gets done.

A Stage 2 contribution is *self-focused*, and the approach is primarily *tactical*. Their work environment is structured, helping them understand the expectations of their role. It is at this

Stage where they develop a deep level of expertise in their functional area.

They manage their own time and their own work with minimal guidance or supervision and are rewarded for their competence and capability.

Peer relationships become increasingly important at this Stage, especially in a team context, where they must willingly share information and collaborate with fellow team members to meet objectives. Stage 2 is a great place to be. The work environment is typically structured. They are trusted because they have earned credibility. They are good at what they do, they are recognized as professionals in their industry, and they understand how to get the work done and do it well.

A Shift in Expectations

Experienced Stage 2 individual contributors are expected to transition to Stage 3 at around eight years into their careers due to their experience, expertise, deep understanding of the organization, and ability to deal with complex problems. This expectation can vary by industry and the individual. Some are expected to make this transition much sooner.

If they anticipate these changing expectations, recognize them, and act upon them, their perceived value and impact will skyrocket as individual contributors. If they do not adjust, the exact opposite will likely happen.

Of course, this shift in expectations can also come because of a promotion where they are formally responsible for leading and directing the work of others.

STAGE 3 – LEADING OTHERS

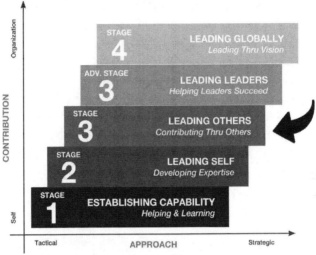

The Key Accountabilities of Stage 3 include:

- ◆ Make sense of work
- ◆ Organize work
- ◆ Build strategic relationships
- ◆ Continuous improvement
- ◆ Develop self and others

The contribution expectation for Stage 3 is focused on *Organization* (or others), and the approach expectation is *Strategic*.

Making the transition to Stage 3 is not as intuitive as the previous transition; it is considered the most difficult transition most people will make in their entire careers.

One reason for this is the Stage 2 behaviors that helped define them as a professional and made them successful in their careers can ultimately get in the way of their progress to Stage 3.

If you take a Stage 3 approach, you will coach others, helping them be more productive and successful, including those new to the organization who need help acclimating to their new surroundings. You will help facilitate their transition from Stage 1 to Stage 2 faster and more seamlessly.

You will build reciprocal relationships both across and higher in the organization while recognizing those relationships as a powerful vehicle to help get work done.

As you make this transition, others will come to you when they need help and guidance. At this point, you have developed the ability to find resources and bring them back to the team. You have also learned how to navigate the political landscape in your company.

You provide direction, vision, and motivation for others by helping them understand the value and meaning of the work they are engaged in, along with why it matters to the success of the team and the company.

You can make this transition as an individual contributor, an informal leader, or a formal manager.

It can take a significant amount of time for those who successfully transition from Stage 2 to Stage 3. Our research indicates that without help, the transition may take you more than three years. But, with appropriate guidance and support, you can make this difficult transition in 12 months or less.

By "guidance and support," I mean exposing you to this

Framework, soliciting help from your manager, a coach, or a mentor, and then working with them through observation and feedback.

You must gain an awareness of the new expectations and willingly change to meet them. Someone (your direct manager is the ideal candidate) needs to hold you accountable for taking a Stage 3 approach and making a Stage 3 contribution. This includes making sure you are responsible for more leadership-oriented activities and outcomes.

> **KEY POINT:** *To be an effective manager, transition to Stage 3. If you decide not to be a manager, you should still consider this same transition.*

Examples: A Stage 2 Manager and a Stage 3 Manager

A *Stage 2 Manager* is someone in a formal manager role who is expected to meet the leadership expectations of Stage 3 but has not yet transitioned. Remember the premature promotion issue we discussed? Here is a perfect example.

Carol is a long-time Emerge Leadership Group consultant and business partner. She shares her personal experience as a Stage 2 Manager. Carol's story is fascinating because it is unusual. It contains two parts; both reveal compelling lessons. As she tells her story, keep in mind what you have learned so far regarding the Stages of Impact Framework.

Here is Carol, in her own words:

"I found that I loved helping people learn and became a trainer at a large financial company. I had been an individual contributor in customer service and sales and now trained others in that role.

"I was in the role formerly as a trainer for approximately one year when my boss asked me what I might like to do in the future. I told him I wanted his job. I think I said that because I felt like that's what I should say, as a 29-year-old in the financial industry.

"I got his job. And although he was an awesome boss – providing feedback and counsel regularly – I was entirely unprepared for managing a group of trainers at this level in the company. I reported directly to the General Manager at the location.

"I loved helping people learn, and since we were short-handed, and I was unclear about what I needed to do as a manager, I put myself in the classroom as much as possible. I micro-managed. I didn't manage. My direct reports would be upset with me, and I didn't understand why. I was so miserable that I told the General Manager I wanted to demote myself back to a trainer. Doing this was unheard of. But he let me do it."

Carol was a solid, capable, and respected Stage 2 individual contributor. If not, she likely would have never received the promotion in the first place. But when promotions happen, expectations change immediately. Carol, a once-respected individual contributor, was now an irritating manager. Others expected her to behave differently, in more of a *Stage 3 way*. She was bright enough to recognize the disconnect and did the right thing by asking to go back. She was also lucky enough to have a manager who realized the error, got creative, and made something happen to keep her. Like she said, "doing this was unheard of." Now, back to our story:

"After being a trainer for some time, I willingly chose to become a manager again, with three direct reports who did very different jobs that I had never done before. They also happened to be friends and peers. So, because I couldn't contribute expertise, I listened to what they needed, provided resources, shared my network, made sure they were visible to those who would help them accomplish their work, and coached them in their interactions with others. I loved my job as their manager."

Carol was fortunate to have a second chance. She shared with us how this time, she had earned the respect of her peers before she was promoted—not just from a technical expertise standpoint, but they respected her as a leader. Her boss had given her opportunities to lead. She had performed well, to the point where everyone on the team fully expected Carol to be selected when the position became available. She had earned "leadership credibility" by acting in a Stage 3 way before she was promoted.

I should highlight another important lesson: Carol could not micromanage or control work she did not know how to complete. This situation forced her to observe, listen, and understand. Most importantly, she had to let go and trust her people to do what they said they would do.

Recycling

There is a concept we refer to as *Recycling*, and you should become familiar with it as you consider management as a potential career option.

Let's suppose Jane is a frontline IT manager. She has

been in her role for three years, and her boss's manager asks her to take on a new assignment in a different part of the organization. Jane will be helping a struggling team whose manager did a poor job and recently left the company for another opportunity.

Jane will be functioning in a similar role doing the same thing she is currently doing, but with a different team. Let's assume she has transitioned to Stage 3. When Jane moves over to the new team, what happens to her from a Stages standpoint? Even though Jane is Stage 3 and knows the role and company, she must still go back or recycle through Stage 1. Why? Because the team dynamics, team culture, and individual team members are different. Jane needs to allow at least 2-3 months of getting to know her new surroundings, taking a Stage 1 approach, then a Stage 2 approach, and finally back to Stage 3 where she can begin to make a positive impact.

Suppose her desire to prove her credibility is too strong. She rushes in and makes decisions when there is still a lot she doesn't know. Jane can unintentionally hurt her credibility, damage morale, and slow productivity from an already battered team.

ADVANCED STAGE 3 – LEADING LEADERS

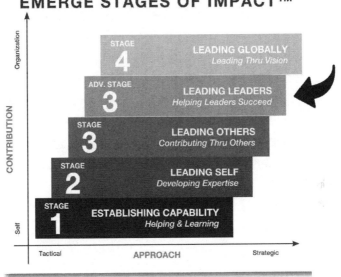

Let's move on to the next Stage. An Advanced Stage 3 – Leading Leaders' approach and contribution are expected of those who manage other managers. These leaders play a vital role in the organization. They are often close enough to the organizational leaders to understand the company's strategic direction and close enough to where the actual work happens to help ensure alignment occurs between them.

They must excel at identifying and selecting talent to fill leadership positions and then help those individuals navigate the challenging transition to Stage 3 by holding them accountable for leadership work. Doing this helps supercharge the entire company.

They are keenly aware of where they spend their time and strive to stay focused on those activities which drive the most value. They leverage relationships to help facilitate the horizontal flow of ideas, information, and resources back and forth across group boundaries (silos).

They work at driving decision-making and risk-taking down to lower levels of the organization and foster strategic thinking with their direct reports and others.

A common question asked about this Stage is why we call it Advanced Stage 3 instead of Stage 4, which seems more intuitive. The best way to answer this question is to look back at the transition from Stage 2 to Stage 3 (p 101-105). This transition is mostly about letting go of the behaviors, the approach, and the contribution, that made the person successful as an individual contributor.

But the transition from Stage 3 to Advanced Stage 3 is different. Review the Key Accountabilities of Stage 3 – Leading Others (p 103). You will discover that those behaviors need to be maintained rather than let go, because they strengthen the individual attempting to move to Advanced Stage 3. This transition is more about adding on or building upon what made them successful rather than letting go.

In other words, it is still Stage 3, but it is at a higher level of complexity. The approach still needs to be strategic – only more so. And the contribution still needs to be organization (others) oriented – only more so.

STAGE 4 – LEADING GLOBALLY

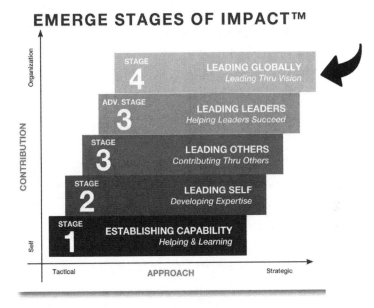

The Key Accountabilities of Stage 4 include:

◆ Represents the organization to the outside
◆ Initiates and supports organizational programs
◆ Formulates organization-wide practices
◆ Directs resources towards strategic goals
◆ Provides organizational direction

Finally, Stage 4. This Stage constitutes the smallest number of individuals in the company, occupying senior-level positions like CEO or Business Unit Leader. They need to provide vision and guidance for the entire organization.

Leading Globally does not refer to a geographical location but rather to the overall business. Their approach must be primarily strategic, and their contribution must be focused on the organization. They must also recognize and understand the impact of the strategic decisions they make. These decisions will determine the long-term health of the organization for the foreseeable future.

This transition is a difficult one to make. These leaders must shift from an internal focus (functions, groups, and individuals) to an external focus on what is happening in the marketplace and where the company fits into it.

In most cases, roles with Stage 4 expectations are entirely different from the roles they have been accustomed to so far in their careers. For example, someone who has spent the last 20 years in various leadership positions in finance will find it challenging not to favor finance over other functions. It is common and natural for them to think and make strategic decisions in financial terms.

Continuing with the example above, to successfully transition to Stage 4, they would not be required to give up the experience and value their background in finance gives them. Rather, they need to recognize and appreciate the various support functions and groups in the entire organization. The needs of the organization take precedence over the needs of any individual or group of individuals.

They must develop relationships with those individuals or entities that could impact or dramatically influence the company in any way. These include key stockholders, key customers, key vendors, government entities, etc.

QUESTIONS TO ASK ABOUT YOUR TRANSITION

As we close our discussion on the Stages of Impact Framework, hopefully, you see the critical nature of making a transition to Stage 3. Reflect on what you have learned and ask yourself the following questions related to this topic:

The Transition to Stage 3

- How does my behavior illustrate that I am aware of the need to transition to Stage 3?
- What are the most critical leadership skills I can acquire for the role I am considering?
- What types of relationships and with whom do I need to develop them to increase my influence in the organization?
- How can I begin to broaden and lengthen my time perspective considering the long-term impact of our work as a team?
- How can I begin to value the kinds of activities that involve working with people?

Contribution

- In what ways could I consider others and the potential impact I have on them in the process of doing my work?
- Do I think about my actions and the impact they have on others upstream/downstream?

- What can I do to help others be more effective in what they need to accomplish?
- In what ways am I too focused on my task list—the stuff I am working on and what I must get done?

Approach

- In what ways could I take more of a Stage 3 approach to my day-to-day work activities?
- What do I need to do to begin to make a mindset shift to be more in line with Stage 3?

CONTENT APPLICATION STORY

"I Want to Be a Manager!" (Part 4)

Part 3 Review

In the previous chapter, Jacob met with Adeline at the end of his project. Although the project was completed on time and to the stakeholders' satisfaction, many of Adeline's outcomes she expected to see from Jacob were not met.

Adeline offered to construct another opportunity, this time, with some additional clarity around the leadership expectations.

Part 4 Continuation

Jacob stood at the door of Adeline's office at the appointed time, unable to hide his anticipation as he wondered what she had cooked up for him.

"Come on in and have a seat." Adeline motioned to one of the three chairs surrounding a small round glass-topped table positioned in the corner of her office. "I have been looking forward to our meeting." She pulled up a chair opposite Jacob.

"How do you feel about everything since we last met?" Adeline asked.

"Pretty good," Jacob said. "I've been thinking a lot about what you told me—reflecting on the whole project experience. It was tough to get your feedback and to hear how the team viewed my performance. I was upset and in denial for quite a while before I started to process it, and although I am still not completely clear, I think I'm beginning to understand at least some of what you shared with me."

Adeline was pleased that he had been able to move past the blame game and start looking at how his behavior and approach had a big part in how things had worked out.

"Here is what I have in mind." Adeline pulled some documents out of a folder. "I will email a copy of all of this when we finish our meeting."

She spread several pages out on the table.

"One of my boss's peers has a high-profile project she is organizing. I've made arrangements for you to participate in it. You will not be running the project, but you will be playing an important part."

Jacob looked doubtful. "How am I supposed to learn to be a leader without being the leader?"

Adeline smiled, "Leadership is not just about being the boss – the one in charge."

She paused, opened her laptop, and began typing. "A close colleague of mine showed me a *Leadership Expectations Framework called the Stages of Impact*.[28] They use it in their company to visually explain what I have been attempting to illustrate for you."

Adeline turned the laptop for Jacob to see. The words *Stages of Impact* and a series of rectan-  gle-shaped boxes stacked on top of one another filled the screen. "Here is the Framework – the model I have been looking for," she said.

Adeline referred to some notes she had taken. The Framework suggested the necessity of moving from one Stage to another over time.

They worked through the Framework together, spending most of the time on the details of the move or transition from Stage 2 (Leading Self) to Stage 3 (Leading Others), which would be the expectation for Jacob.

As their conversation continued, Jacob focused intensely, the wheels turning in his head.

Adeline connected what they had been discussing in the Framework to the assignment she was giving him by saying, "Let's talk about the outcomes I would like to see with this project. Because you will not be the project manager, the demands on your time should not be as intense, allowing you to apply more focus on some of these leadership capabilities."

Jacob nodded and then leaned forward in his chair, eager to hear what she had in mind.

Referring to Stage 3 of the Stages of Impact Framework, Adeline said, "I would like you to focus on some outcomes related to a couple of these *Key Accountabilities*."

"First, I want you to work on *building relationships* with others on this project team. Get to know them. Be interested in them and learn about their backgrounds, experience, and expertise. Be inquisitive about the role they will play in this project. Listen to what they have to say!'

"Find out how you can help them get what they need. These are bright people with bright futures in our company. Make the kind of connections that will result in long-term relationships with them. The challenge will be *how* you do this given everyone is so busy.'

"Next, I want you to seek to understand *why* we are working on this project. Find out how it helps us meet our strategic objectives. And I would like you to share how you believe it aligns with our company's vision and mission. They call it *Make Sense of Work* in the Stages of Impact Framework. It is a skill you need to develop to help others maintain purpose and meaning in their work—helping them stay engaged in what you, as a team, are working on."

"And finally, I want you to work with Yegor."

Yegor was a direct report of Adeline's and a peer on Jacob's team.

"He has been struggling to get up-to-speed on the new data analytics software we installed several months ago. You know it well. I want you to coach him in a way that does not make him feel more foolish than he does already. See if you can build him up, find where his strengths are."

Jacob nodded in agreement.

"Your challenge, Jacob, will be letting him struggle a little and make a few mistakes without you jumping in to save him.

"I will commit to meet with you more frequently than I did on the last project to give you more immediate help and feedback where you need it," Adeline concluded.

Jacob seemed genuinely excited. "I have some additional questions I need to ask you and information I need to gather, but I'm all in! When do I start?"

(To be continued in the next chapter)

➤ CHAPTER FIVE
MANAGEMENT BLINDSPOTS

MANAGEMENT BLINDSPOTS

I remember thinking I was pretty hot stuff as I slid my laminated driver's license into my wallet and walked out of the Department of Transportation building. I was a brand new sixteen-year-old driver, not the typical, average sixteen-year-old driver, but one who had failed the driver's test so many times, my friends began to make fun of me.

To combat the ridicule, I decided to announce to everyone that I knew more than all of them about driving simply because of the number of hours of study and preparation I had put into passing the test. I certainly knew more than any of my friends. I was full of confidence. But that confidence only lasted for a week.

While driving to work early one morning, I merged onto the freeway, and because I was late, I decided to move into the left lane so I could travel with the faster-moving traffic. I glanced up into the overhead rearview mirror to check for cars behind me. No concerns there. Then, I looked out at the left driverside rearview mirror. The coast was clear. So, I pushed the blinker lever down, signaling left, and started to move into the fast lane.

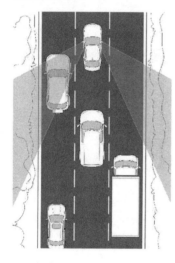

My action caused a very loud and prolonged horn blast from a car I did not see, a car that was in my *blindspot*. Of course, I jerked the wheel back to the right as an angry-looking middle-aged hothead driver mouthed some words that I could not hear but fully understood, followed by an obscene gesture. I wanted to return the favor but thought better of it.

I learned several valuable lessons that day.

- ◆ First, I did not know as much as I thought I did about driving.
- ◆ Second, I discovered what a blindspot was. An area that I could not see by looking at both mirrors.
- ◆ Third, I realized I needed to *physically turn my head and look over my left shoulder to check my blindspot* before changing lanes (that information was probably in the drivers' training handbook. I just didn't remember it).

The purpose of this chapter is to provide you with a few *management blindspots*. These issues can create real problems if you are not aware of them.

Regardless of whether or not each blindspot directly applies to you, it will be helpful to become familiar with each of them if you are to become a high-impact leader.

> **Note:** This chapter will simply make you aware of these blindspots. It will not provide you with solutions and strategies for dealing with those you feel may be obstacles to your transition.

IDENTITY CRISIS

As stated earlier in this book, a primary reason for new manager dissatisfaction is misaligned expectations. This blindspot – *identity crisis*, is a prime example of this problem. Although not as common as the others in this chapter, it is worth discussing.

What I mean by *identity crisis* is this: Some managers consider themselves managers in title only. For example, I occasionally run into a manager who doesn't feel the need to transition. When I describe what must be done to move to Stage 3, they smile, shake their head, and tell me their circumstances are different. Their top priority is to be a superstar individual contributor delivering the outstanding technical/functional work their team expects from them. The leadership and management stuff will be done once their more important work is finished.

There you have it, a manager with misaligned expectations—a manager with an identity crisis. Interestingly, when I discuss the conversation with their manager, they are often surprised. The priority has always been the other way around. The primary objective is to be an effective leader! A leader with some individual contributor assignments to complete after the management and leadership responsibilities are handled.

Be aware that culture can play a big part in promoting this issue. Highly technical organizations like research and development (R&D) labs are notorious for downplaying the importance of leadership. Technical prowess rules the day.

Also, keep in mind that it is natural and easy to fall for this blindspot if you love your technical/functional work.

KEY POINT: *Many managers unwittingly train their people to treat them as the Stage 2 superstar, the expert, the go-to person. It is seductive, and the tragedy is they do it to themselves, making it almost impossible to transition to Stage 3 and a higher level of leadership effectiveness.*

MANAGING FORMER PEERS

Are you considering a position where you will manage former peers? If you prepare in advance and expectations are appropriately set with the team, it should be a great experience. Part of that preparation includes transitioning to Stage 3, so your peers are not surprised by the promotion. If you do not prepare in advance, it could be a miserable experience.

As I reflect on the work I have done with thousands of

new leaders through the years, this group, by far, is the most battered and beaten. They are the most wide-eyed and eager to learn. They have the most legitimate questions. Why? Because they did not see this blindspot coming until they ran headlong into it!

Managing your peers may seem like a dream job. I mean, you know these people. You are familiar with their strengths and weaknesses. You may even hang out with them on weekends and holidays. At first blush, you may wonder if there is a downside?

For instance, let's assume you are the manager. The company invests in new automation equipment, substantially increasing product output. As the boss, you must seek to understand the purposes of this change and communicate it to your team. You learn that part of the change will require a headcount reduction of 15%.

Even though you did not make the decision, you must support it, and doing so will cause your peers to see you in a different light from now on. How will you socialize at the club with the crew after letting two of them go the previous week?

The following story illustrates some additional challenges and opportunities related to this potential blindspot.

Penny – A 'Managing Former Peers' Example

Penny is a skilled software engineer with a passion for back-end design work. She has always had a natural desire to help others with complex issues and quickly developed a reputation as a talented professional. Her peers would come to her regularly, causing her to fall behind on her work. Still, because of her quality focus and personal capability, she would work additional hours on her own time to get it done.

Penny was a good collaborator and enjoyed sharing the credit of good work outcomes with others. Her peers liked and respected her, and with these qualities, she was recognized as the top choice when the team manager position became available. Initially, she did very well, working with four direct reports, two in the home office where she is based and two overseas.

The challenges began to surface as customer demands and timelines became tighter. When the team met their deadlines, everything was fine. But when they fell short, she would catch heat from her boss for not delivering on time.

Holding her former peers, who were now her direct reports, accountable for getting work done on time had become almost unbearable. It was not in Penny's nature to have to come down on someone for a performance problem, and *the fact that these people were her friends made it doubly difficult.*

She despised the tough conversations, and because they were creating so much intense anxiety in her life, she had finally decided that management was not for her. She was going to quit her job.

Penny and her family are friends of ours. I happened to be talking to her husband one day, and I asked how she was doing. He told me about her promotion and mentioned Penny had barely been in the position six months and was already considering leaving. He said she had decided management did not suit her.

I asked him if he thought she would mind if I called and talked to her about it. He thought it was a great idea.

A few days later, I sent Penny a text message and offered to talk about her situation. She immediately responded that she was anxious to discuss it with me. Our conversation went something like this:

"Hi Penny, I heard about your promotion. And I also understand you're thinking about leaving?"

She laughed, "Yeah, I've been thinking about it a lot lately. I think I'm ready to jump back into my old work – I feel like I am better suited for it—I'm good at it, I enjoy it, and I will be able to focus my efforts on my craft. I've recognized a harsh reality about this management thing—it is over my head; I don't feel like I know what I'm doing."

As she talked, I sensed that Penny genuinely wanted to be a successful manager, but she did not believe she had the skillset. She was undoubtedly correct. Most people lack those skills when they first move into a management position. She had only been there for six months. Success comes with patience, self-awareness, a willingness to develop new skills, and a focused determination to learn from past mistakes and become better over time.

I asked, "Do you enjoy any part of it? Did you have some positive outcomes?

"Of course!" she replied. She described her passion for the kind of work her company does and about organizing projects in a way that matches the capabilities of those best suited for specific responsibilities. She also spoke about the satisfaction of team efforts coming together to successful completion.

I shifted the conversation, "So what isn't so great? What don't you like that is causing you to think about leaving?"

She rattled off a few things—primarily minor process frustrations. But the tenor of the conversation changed when she started talking about working with her direct reports.

"These people were my former peers, my friends. We had a lot of fun working together. Now it's awkward. It's like they are all trying to avoid me. I'm not part of the group anymore. I sense resentment from them—especially from Greg."

"Penny, what you are going through is very common, and most people who are in positions similar to yours face similar difficulties," I said.

"Here is what you need to know: The awkwardness will likely take care of itself over time. But you can take a few actions now that will make a big difference. First, I recommend you meet with them either as a team or one-on-one, whichever is most comfortable.

"Acknowledge the obvious weirdness of having to move from being one of the pals to becoming their boss. Let them talk about how they feel and solicit what you can do to be supportive. Make clear that although you will always be their friend, the fundamental relationship has and will continue to change. Then ask for their support. It will surprise you how much better it will be just by acknowledging the *elephant in the room*—the big obvious uncomfortable problem that no one wants to address."

"I like that. I will give it a try." Penny said.

"Now, let's talk about this Greg character," I continued.

"He sounds like he may have some additional issues that we need to consider. Tell me more about his situation."

"Well," Penny began. "Greg has been a huge challenge. We worked well together in the past, but when I became the manager, it all changed. He tries to push my buttons—to aggravate me. For instance, he works wacky hours. He leaves me stressing about whether he will get his part of the project done on time. I try to talk to him about it, but he constantly resists my requests and suggestions—and the conversation gets heated and goes downhill from there," she sighed.

"How is Greg's work performance? Does he get the work done?" I asked.

"That is one of the issues I have with him," she said.

"He works from a home office and kind of comes and goes as he pleases. Some days he is just gone, even when a deadline is closing in. But then he works around the clock and gets it done – occasionally a day behind schedule, which irritates my boss. But he does get it done."

"Would you change your mind about leaving if Greg were out of the picture?" I asked.

Her voice brightened, "Yes!" followed by a hopeful pause.

"Well, I'm not a hitman; I can't just make him disappear. But if we talk through this together, we might discover a different way to approach him and, in the process, make life better for both of you."

She was entirely on board, so I dug a little deeper asking for more specifics about the situation, and here is what I discovered:

Greg was an unusually talented and experienced professional – perhaps the brightest on the team. He had applied for the team manager position, but they selected Penny, an interesting and critical piece of information.

Management Blindspots | 127

I also found out he had been passed over for other leadership positions in the past. I thought there was a good chance Greg felt slighted and possibly a little bitter?

"Let me make sure I understand." I inquired. "If he is one of your best performers, and he completes his work…mostly on time. What is the problem? Does the company require him to work certain hours?"

Penny knew where I was going with this. "Look, I just want him to work like the rest of us do. You know, the 8 am to 5 pm schedule, as a team." She was insistent about this!

"How does the company feel about it?" I pressed. "Do they require you to work certain hours? Or do they just want the work to get done right and on time?"

"Meeting the deadline—and done correctly are the primary objectives. But it is just not right, all of us are working regular hours, and Greg is not."

"Do you or members of the team need him to be there during those hours?"

"Occasionally, but not typically."

"Do you have many impromptu calls or unscheduled collaboration meetings?"

"Rarely."

It became evident to me the way Penny was approaching Greg was a big part of the problem. She was a classic micromanager.

"Penny, can I make another recommendation? Let go of your need to control Greg's schedule. Tell him you recognize and trust him as a top-rate professional. Make him feel important and then give him the freedom he wants. Let him know he owns his part of the work. He can do it whenever and however he wants – if he commits to meet the project deadlines. It is on him. Then see what happens. You have nothing to lose, Penny; he is doing it like this anyway." There was a long pause. I could tell Penny was seriously considering it.

Before she responded, I added: "I would also encourage you to look for every opportunity to genuinely compliment him, especially when he does something well and when he gets it done on time. I think you will see a difference."

By the time we ended the conversation, Penny was genuinely excited. She was anxious to try out the ideas we discussed.

About a month later, she sent me the following text message:

> *"Hi Sheldon, I appreciate your suggestions. I have learned to accept my rebel employee's style of doing things. Greg does not work the way I think he should but giving him his freedom has made a huge difference. He still goes 2-3 days without doing anything and then, 'BAM!' he does an all-nighter and catches up. He drives me crazy, but I must admit, he is a genius. He just helped solve a major issue today and finished his project on time—once again, at the very last minute—but he completed it on time."*
>
> *"Oh, and one more thing, I have decided to stay in the Team Manager role. I am not going to quit! This has turned out to be a great learning experience for me and has provided some needed career growth. Thanks again! Penny"*

I was thrilled to receive this news. I appreciated Penny's efforts and that she didn't give up. I could tell she wanted this to work, and it did.

About 11 months later, I saw Penny and her family at a

social gathering and asked how things were going with Greg and how she felt about her job. She was so excited to talk to me about it. We scheduled a phone call, and here is what she shared with me:

"When I started to think about how Greg had changed, I realized that it had more to do with the *adjustments I made in my behavior. I was the problem.* I tried to build even more trust with him and continued to *call out* his accomplishments and protect him when he occasionally made a mistake. I could tell that Greg was deeply impressed by these actions.

"What began as an intense, unpleasant relationship had grown into a comfortable, trusting one. I even began to lobby management to give Greg a promotion, and they did! It was amazing. Here was a guy who was passed over multiple times before, and now he's at the same level as I am. Greg recognized the part I played in this and has shown a lot of gratitude toward me.

"Realizing how well this worked for Greg, I began to pay more attention to the strengths and weaknesses of my other direct reports. I focused on building relationships with them, striving to help them improve their skills and productivity. It has been rewarding to see them more engaged.

"Oh, and you will never guess. Management promoted another one of my direct reports! Now, *everyone is referring to me as a people developer.* I would have never described myself in this way, but I must admit it has been immensely gratifying. I am so glad I decided to stay in my role.

"I should mention one more important thing. My boss

has been a great support. He has pushed me to do some uncomfortable things, and those experiences are giving me confidence in my ability to be a good manager."

I share this story as an illustration of the positive results which can occur as you step up and do hard things—working through unfamiliar and uncomfortable situations, including, for some, managing former peers.

In Walt Disney/Pixar's animated film *Finding Nemo*,[29] there is a clownfish named Marlin. He has lost his young son, Nemo, who was captured by some fishermen. Marlin embarks on an extraordinary journey to find Nemo. The quest is fraught with endless danger, and at one point, he unexpectedly gets caught in the middle of a forest of deadly jellyfish. In a sheer panic, he bounces his way through, but not without injury. He is stung into unconsciousness.

Sometime later, he slowly wakes up, finding himself riding on the back of a giant sea turtle named Crush, who is with a group of other turtles speeding along on the East Australian Current. Crush is awed by what he saw Marlin bravely encounter and survive. Marlin asks, "What happened?" Crush responds, "I saw the whole thing, …you, mini-man, takin' on the jellies… you got serious thrill issues, dude!"

You might feel like Marlin at times as you navigate your way through your forest of jellyfish, wondering about your own set of serious thrill issues. But with some coaching, development, and time, you can turn most of your challenging situations into great learning experiences. The fact Penny is doing this, one day at a time, "taking on the jellies" (difficult situations) and developing skills in the process is a remarkable accomplishment.

> **KEY POINT:** *Moving from being one of the "buddies" who socialize together to being the boss is more complicated than most realize.*

THE WORKING MANAGER

Most first-line managers are what we call 'working managers.' The definition of a working manager is *someone who has management responsibilities who is also required to do a certain amount of individual contributor duties* – often the same kinds of activities and responsibilities of their direct reports.

It can feel a little out-of-control as you learn to manage the hopping back and forth from doing to leading. The percentage split (management vs. technical/functional work) can vary widely. In most cases, the scale tends to favor the individual contributor's responsibilities side, making the role of a working manager a challenging one and prompting the saying:

"*I'm so busy doing; I don't have the time to lead.*"

> **KEY POINT:** *The demand on your time as a working manager will be as difficult a challenge as you will likely ever face; it can bury you.*

Learning to take a Stage 3 approach as you deal with this dilemma will help you make a more significant impact and allow you to enjoy a measure of work-life balance.

The following blindspots contribute to the working manager challenge.

No Position Backfill

There are circumstances where the ability to backfill the position you just vacated does not happen. Sometimes it is by design, and then there are other times when budgets get cut in the middle of your promotion. Now, you have the new role's management requirements and leadership expectations on top of your former full-time individual contributor responsibilities—a rough situation any way you look at it.

Communication Overload

Because of your new position, you will receive, with few exceptions, a significant increase in email and other communications. New managers claim they suddenly find themselves in the deep end of the pool, swimming in hundreds of new emails each day.

You will need to incorporate some coping strategies to manage this deluge, or it will dominate your time and attention. You will find yourself increasingly unproductive as you constantly pop in and out of your inbox, interrupting your ability to focus time and effort on strategic approaches to your work and your team.

Meeting Mania

Expect to see a significant increase in the meetings you will be invited or required to attend. Depending on the organization's culture, you will spend a large portion of your day running from one meeting to the next, making it difficult to do what you need to do as a manager. We consistently hear stories of first-line managers up late, night after night, trying to punch through their exploding email inbox because they have been in endless meetings all day and have had little time to respond to much of anything.

Bennett – A Working Manager Example

I share the following story with you to illustrate how complex the working manager challenge can be, and yet, at the same time, how rewarding it is if approached in the right way.

I began coaching Bennett when he worked as an individual contributor in Supply Chain for one of the largest public water and power utilities in North America. He wisely began preparing for a potential opportunity long before one came available. When the creation of a new Lead Supervisor position popped up, he was ready. He applied for it and received the promotion.

He was given four direct reports and was responsible for overall team productivity, organizing and assigning work, coaching, developing, holding performance reviews, helping to determine raises, and more.

In one of my conversations with Bennett, I asked him to think about his reasons for deciding to go into management. He thought about it for a few moments and then said:

"I had worked for my company for nine years when one of my co-workers who was also a good friend became my boss. I was nervous about how this would affect our relationship, and it was awkward at first, but he handled the move so well and did such a good job it inspired me to do the same thing—to be a manager.

"I wanted to be like him, to have a positive influence on others. So, this was one of the initial reasons."

"Were there other drivers helping to push you there?" I asked.

"Yes, there was. I was good at my job, and I just felt like I could take on more responsibility.

"This was a newly created role, allowing me to still report to my existing boss and manage some of my former peers. We were a great team. I cared about these people. I wanted to help them be successful, and I felt like I had their respect and confidence.

"Money was certainly important to me, and of course, the increase in credibility and status a position like this generated was a plus.

"I also wanted to have the ability to make a difference at a higher level. I could see so many processes we could improve. I had streamlined my workload, and I wanted to help others do the same.

"Lastly, I wanted to try to help influence the direction of the organization, to have the opportunity to be involved in the decisions to help our company move forward in a positive way – the thought of this was exciting to me."

Bennett had a healthy batch of motives giving him a reinforced foundation that he needed for the difficulties ahead.

I then asked some additional questions. "When you stepped into the role, what did you find more complicated than you thought it would be? What weren't you prepared for?"

He responded: "Delegation is difficult for me – much more than I thought it would be. It has been hard to let go of things I like and want to do. I've been doing them for so long; they have become my identity—who I am.

"But I would say the biggest shock for me was the tough conversations I have had to have. To be clear, I knew they would take place. I just didn't realize how difficult they would be for me.

"I was under the assumption that we (my colleagues/team members) were professionals and were respectful of each other. I found out this was not entirely accurate.

"One individual, whom I had known for years, became extremely emotional over an issue, to the point of yelling and screaming. I was stunned – I didn't know what to do. I involved my manager, and he helped me in a big way!

"I discovered an additional surprise. I had no idea how much time this job would require. I took on the new role and did not have the luxury of hiring a replacement for my old job. I had to do both. It was crazy difficult!

"The number of meetings I was being asked to attend – an average of four hours every day! It was insane. Half of them appeared to me to be a waste of my time.

"Now, for some good news, I shared my concern about these meetings with my boss. And this goes to show how amazing he is—he agreed with my assessment and helped me get *uninvited* to a number of them so I could focus more on growing the effectiveness of my team."

"This is quite the list of challenges, Bennett. Now, what about the good stuff? What about this experience has been rewarding for you?"

He thought for a moment. "These experiences have changed me – in a good way. They have helped me have more tolerance and compassion for people. I have realized it is not only about me, driving hard to get my work done. It is more about helping my team.

"I have learned to slow down, work through issues, try to understand where my direct reports are coming from, and seek to balance the needs of the individual with the needs of the business.

"One personally rewarding experience happened when I found out a member of my team had decided to leave the company. I worked through the issue with her, helped her explore alternatives, and encouraged her to see that her situation was not as hopeless as she thought. She decided to stay. This experience was incredibly gratifying to me!

"Another thing, exposure to upper-level management, getting to know them, and building a relationship of trust with them has been amazing. Now, these executives come to me and ask my opinion on important issues facing the company. Having the ability to influence the direction of not only the team but the organization has been wonderful!"

I end this story with Bennett's final statement to me. It answers the question you may be grappling with at this point in your journey. I asked him if taking the management path had been worth it. It sounded like a lot of work, unnecessary meetings, painful conversations, and extra time spent for no additional compensation. Without the slightest hesitation, he responded:

> *"This role has been the most rewarding experience of my entire career."*

KEY POINT: *Those who choose the management path for the right reasons and approach it the right way will experience tremendous rewards and provide value to their team and organization in the process!*

LOOKING FOR MANAGEMENT BLINDSPOTS

Here are questions for you to consider about the topics in this chapter. By asking and acting on them, you will be more prepared to deal with them when they arise.

- Do I understand what an *identity crisis* is in the context of this book? How will I make sure I know what my expectations are before accepting a new position? In what ways will I "let go" of my need to be the technical/functional expert?
- Will I have to *manage former peers* in the position I am considering? Do I ever participate in negative talk about management with my peers? If yes, how can I be more supportive, realizing that someday I may be in the manager's chair? What are some additional ways I can prepare for this experience ahead of time?
- Usually, those who are in first-line manager roles will

also be *working managers*. How can I best deal with this issue? In what ways can I begin to transition to Stage 3 now? How can I change my approach to my work long before a management opportunity becomes available?
- Is the *'no position backfill'* issue a possibility with the role I am considering? How can I get ready beforehand, so I do not have to scramble at the last minute to deal with this blindspot?
- *Communication overload.* What kinds of strategies could I employ regarding email management? What unhealthy cultural issues related to communications are there that I could help rectify?
- Is *meeting mania* a problem at my company? How can I understand the purpose of these meetings? In what ways might I gain permission to be uninvited to those that do not provide sufficient value for me to attend?

CONTENT APPLICATION STORY: THE CONCLUSION

"I Want to Be a Manager!" (Part 5)

Part 4 Review

We left Part 4 with Jacob taking on a new set of assignments. He and Adeline reviewed the Stages of Impact Leadership Framework, which helped her communicate the expectations she had for him. It also helped Jacob understand what he needed to do to meet those expectations and their associated outcomes.

Part 5 Conclusion

Jacob reflected on that first meeting when he approached his boss, Adeline, demanding a management position.

Jacob remembered how frustrated he was when the promotion he wanted didn't materialize.

As he reflected on the experience, he appreciated Adeline's firmness as she resisted his demands. He also respected the way she had shown empathy and had been patient with him.

Then something else occurred to him, "Was there even an open position for him to move into at the time?" He didn't think so, but if there were, and Adeline had given in and promoted him…Whoa! He shook his head at the thought! It would have been a disaster!

When Adeline suggested a development opportunity, a project, where he could show everyone how good he was, he jumped at the chance.

Adeline allowed him to struggle and even fail in some areas. He learned much from this experience, not the least of which was some humility. He also believed Adeline had learned some valuable lessons as well.

The second leadership opportunity had been a much different experience. With the use of a leadership expectations framework called The Stages of

Impact, Adeline explained, in greater clarity, what she expected from him. This vision, coupled with the Stages of Impact framework, made a remarkable difference in how he thought about these new assignments. He valued them more than he had the first time around.

He approached them in a much more strategic way. Instead of focusing on himself and learning from experience, his attention was more long-term and others oriented. He thought about the impact he and his team members would potentially have on others upstream and downstream based upon their actions and decisions.

For example, one of the assignments Adeline had given him was to work on a project of one of her boss's peers. Instead of leading the project, she wanted him to focus on getting to know the other team members in a way he would not have considered otherwise.

He worked hard at this, looking for opportunities to help these peers in any way he could. A few of them had become good friends. There was a level of trust between them he had not experienced before. Several of his team members had introduced him to important people in other parts of the organization. He was beginning to realize the value and impact of solid, trusting, reciprocal relationships.

Adeline sat down with him and reviewed his progress.

"I'm pleased with how far you have come, Jacob!"

"I thought we might go back to our first interview for a moment." She pulled up a document on her computer.

"I asked you what your Primary and Secondary motives were – those driving you to want to be a manager. You told me: *A New Challenge* and a *Pay Raise* were your Primary ones, and your Secondary motives were: *Increased Respect* and *Help Others*. Have those motives changed since then, or would you add any others?"

Jacob pondered the question for a moment. He did feel differently about these new assignments. He genuinely valued some non-technical activities now even more than he did his analytics work, which surprised him in a way. It had not happened quickly, but slowly, almost imperceptibly.

"Yes, I would like to add a few items. First, as my #1 Primary Motive, *Build Strategic Relationships*, and as my #1 Secondary Motive *Coach and Develop Others*."

Jacob told Adeline about his experience working on the project with his peer group. He also told her about what he had been learning working with Yegor. It was much more complicated than he thought it would be. Jacob believed he would be a natural coach with his knowledge and expertise, but he struggled not to jump in and do it for him.

He could tell the experience was good for both of them. He was learning how to be much more patient, letting others figure out more things for themselves. He could tell Yegor learned faster and better that way.

Jacob was also enjoying the relationship he was building with him. In the beginning, it was a little strained, but over time, as they got to know one another and as Jacob began to figure out how he could best help him, it had become something they both valued – more and more with time.

Adeline smiled and added these items to Jacob's Motives list. "This has turned out to be a solid set of motives," she said.

"But there is one thing we haven't discussed yet. Do you remember how I wanted you to strive to understand *why* you and the project team were working on that particular project? To try to understand the ways it helped us meet our strategic objectives and how it aligned with our company's vision and mission?"

Jacob's Updated Motives
Primary
- Build Strategic Relationships
- New Challenge
- Pay Raise

Secondary:
- Coach and Develop Others
- Increased Respect
- Help Others

"Absolutely," Jacob said as he explained how the project aligned by *Making Sense of the Work*[30] (one of the Key Accountabilities of Stage 3) to Adeline. He answered all questions to her complete satisfaction.

"Doing this changed my perspective and my engagement on this project. It is something I will try to do going forward, regardless of whether I'm in a leadership position or not," Jacob said.

Adeline nodded approvingly.

She observed that Jacob had *gained more credibility with key people who had noticed him and his impact as an individual contributor in a non-manager role.*

"Jacob, I believe you are ready now," Adeline said proudly.

"This does not mean you have fully transitioned; there is still some development you need to do. But I can tell you are thinking about things differently, more long-term, and this is a good sign!"

Jacob looked genuinely pleased but in a more humble way than he had in the beginning.

"Thank you," he said. "I appreciate all you have done for me, Adeline.

"For standing your ground when you knew I was not ready. I also appreciate the stretch opportunities and your patience with me. I won't forget this!"

Adeline smiled. "I have some news for you," she said. "One of my peers contacted me. She has a supervisor position opening in 3-4 weeks. Are you interested? She asked about you specifically."

As he thought about it, he wondered if he wanted to take this step. He was enjoying his new perspective and the impact he was having on others. He thought about a people manager role and the added responsibility it would carry. At the same time, he thought about the benefits of being directly involved with people, processes, and decision-making. He had discovered that the greater the challenge you face and overcome, the greater the reward.

> **KEY POINT:** *The greater the challenge you face and overcome, the greater the reward.*

"I would be interested in exploring it," Jacob said. "But I'm not ready to commit yet. I feel like I need to understand the management requirements and the leadership expectations for the role before deciding which path to take."

Would Jacob ultimately take this management opportunity as a Stage 3 manager, or would he continue where he was, getting to do his technical work, and at the same time, bringing tremendous value to the team and the organization as a Stage 3 non-manager?

(End of: "I Want to Be a Manager!" A Classic Business Dilemma)

➤ CHAPTER SIX
CONFESSIONS OF A HIRING MANAGER

A PEEK BEHIND THE CURTAIN

In this section, you will have a unique opportunity to *peek behind the curtain* to observe some hiring and promotion mistakes hiring managers tend to make.

Let us say your boss comes to you and offers you a promotion. Rather than just accepting it at face value, you will now be able to step back and look at the opportunity more objectively. Consider the possibility your boss might be making an incorrect assumption or a classic promotion mistake. Asking some questions related to this content could help you avoid making a poor career choice.

KEY POINT: *Being aware of the mistakes and assumptions driving hiring and promotion decisions will give you a distinct advantage when considering a management position.*

One of the most important observations we have made in the last 20 years is *the immense influence managers of managers have on the transition of their direct reports. They can dramatically accelerate or delay the transition based upon their actions.*

A manager of managers who has a good understanding of the Stages of Impact and what it takes to transition from Stage 2 to Stage 3 has a distinct advantage. The quality and speed of the transition of their direct reports will increase as they consistently hold them accountable for Stage 3 approaches and contribution. Remember, this is the most challenging transition most individuals will ever make in their careers (Stage 2 to Stage 3).

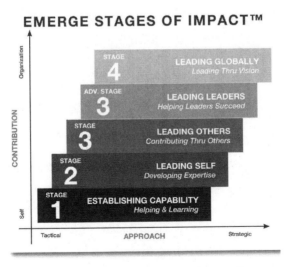

Having a manager who understands this can help reduce transition time from more than three years – to less than one year (depending upon the complexity of the role). The time reduction alone will have a significant impact on the business.

The Selection of First-line Leaders

During the "Maximizing Your Impact"[31] workshop experience for managers of managers, we work on the Key Accountability: *Selects first-line leaders*. I cannot overemphasize the importance of this responsibility! The hiring and promotion decisions these managers make will impact the long-term health of an organization for the foreseeable future. Because of its significance, we incorporate an exercise called *Selection Mistakes and Assumptions*.

Participants are placed in breakout groups and given the task of identifying common mistakes and assumptions they have made as they hire and promote individuals to first-line manager positions. Once they complete their small group work, we bring them back together for a large group discussion. We have compiled a list of the most common mistakes, assumptions, and traps that get them into trouble. This list is what prompted the title of this chapter: "*Confessions of a Hiring Manager.*"

Before sharing these *Confessions*, I should point out the challenging nature of the role of these leaders. They experience tremendous pressure both from above and below. They are literally squeezed in the middle. I have a great deal of respect for what they must deal with day after day.

These leaders have the potential of making a tremendous contribution and impact on the business in a multitude of ways. Yet, like the rest of us, they are prone to make mistakes, especially when faced with intense pressure to deliver timely results in an ever-changing, competitive business environment.

Once I finish sharing these confessions with you, you will have an opportunity to do some self-reflection. I will also give you some questions to ask yourself and ask those offering you or encouraging you to take a manager position.

THE CONFESSIONS
Selecting a top technical/functional performer

Hands down, this is the most common assumption we have encountered, and if you stop and think about it, you can understand why it is such an easy trap to step in. It's logical. Selecting from among the top technical/functional experts makes tremendous sense. These professionals know what quality work looks like and how to get it done in a high-performance way. Although their peers may not always like them, they typically respect them and appreciate that they know the job and what it takes to get it done.

Therefore, according to this *assumption*, these high-performers will help each team member be like them. The choice seems quite obvious!

But when we ask class participants how often this strategy works out, the prevailing answer from nearly every group we have ever worked with is *"about 50% of the time."*

Making a hiring decision by basically flipping a coin is

unwise. You take a massive risk that is simply not worth it. The cost of replacing a manager, as discussed early in this text,[a] is incredibly high. In addition, like Aiden's manager said in the Introduction, "We would have lost twice; first when we lost a great engineer, and second when we lost a manager."[b]

KEY POINT: *Not everyone who is a great athlete makes a great coach. We have all witnessed this. The same principle applies in the business world.*

Time pressure

When most managers get the "green light" to hire or promote someone, the race is on. There is an urgency to fill the position as soon as possible. Why?

- ◆ Budgets can change instantly. If you don't act, you could lose the money set aside for recruiting, hiring, and training a new manager.

- ◆ The new hire's work is likely being shared by already overwhelmed team members – including the boss.
- ◆ Without a leader who provides necessary communication and direction, the team will lose focus, momentum, productivity, and miss deadlines.

---

a   Introduction – Why You Need to Read This Book
b   *Ibid*

150 | Is Management For Me?

For these reasons and others, the emphasis is: *"Fill the position and do it as quickly as possible!"*

Unfortunately, succumbing to rushed decisions because of time pressure raises the probability of creating more problems than necessary. Rushed judgments take more time in the long run, requiring you to backtrack and fix mistakes.

> **KEY POINT:** *Taking the necessary time to do a proper job upfront will save enormous time and money on the backend.*

Longest Tenure

The assumption for this trap goes something like this:

"Let's give the promotion to Glen. He has been around the longest and has been passed over on several previous promotion opportunities. Besides, he deserves it."

There are advantages to utilizing those who have the longest tenure. These folks, like Glen, are great team players, well-liked, and highly competent. They know the organization and how to navigate it to get the work done.

Yet every one of those advantages is an assumption. We don't know for sure (unless we have had the opportunity to observe Glen closely) that any of them are true. But let's assume all of them are accurate. The fact that Glen was previously *passed over* should be a cause for consideration. *There were probably legitimate reasons for it.*

A better solution would be to give Glen some stretch assignments, some opportunities to develop and grow to make sure this is something that both of you want before making a decision.

"We will lose her if we do not promote her"

In Chapter One (pp. 29-30), I shared the story of the sales executive who was about to lose his star salesperson. A competitor was offering her a management position if she would come to work for them. She was ready to walk out the door with her multi-million dollar book of business unless he promoted her. He recognized he would lose no matter which decision he made.

This situation provides the perfect definition for the saying: "I'm caught between a rock and a hard place."

We have observed that most managers of managers who find themselves in similar circumstances tend to give in to the demand and hope they can work around the issues of a poor manager versus having to make up for the lost revenue.

Interestingly, if this sales executive took time to count both the visible and hidden costs of promoting her to a manager position, he might be surprised by the results.

Here are a few examples of the potential fallout if he bends to her demands:

- ◆ He will lose credibility with his other direct reports if he allows her to bully him into giving her what she wants.
- ◆ He will have a difficult time trusting her if she stays. He would undoubtedly be preoccupied with the threat of her walking out the door if she doesn't get what she wants down the road with a different issue.
- ◆ She could create extra work for him as he manages around her Stage 2 approach and behavior.

- She will tend to micromanage, create low engagement, and frustrate her direct reports.
- Her behavior could encourage other high-performers to leave the organization.

And a final thought, there is a high probability that he would not lose *all* the business she is currently managing. Surely, there is a portion of her clients that would remain?

"He reminds me of me"

We also refer to this issue as hiring your clone. The reason people fall for this fallacy is the candidate thinks and sees the world much like the hiring manager. This comfort level makes difficult business decisions more straightforward and much quicker because you agree on most things. Life would be simpler and more manageable. In the complex world we live in, what is not to like about this?

Early in my career, an influential mentor gave me invaluable counsel. He said, "Sheldon, never hire someone like you."

"Why not? I shot back. "Is there something wrong with me?"

He laughed and then said, "Yeah, lots of things. But seriously, you need to surround yourself with people who think differently than you do, who are not afraid to tell you if they believe you are wrong, those who challenge your thinking." He was exactly right!

> **KEY POINT:** *You will almost always make better decisions with others who have a different perspective than you do.*

Settling

Here is the situation with Settling. Let's say that you are the hiring manager. You and a few of your peers just finished interviewing a fresh group of candidates for a frontline supervisor position. When the interviewing is complete, you meet together and agree that none of them made the cut.

But as you talk it through together, the thought of starting the process over again, advertising the position, sorting through each resumé, and then interviewing each member of the new group seems overwhelming. Therefore, as a hiring team, you decide to pick the best candidate among those just interviewed. This action is what we call *Settling*.

Is this a lazy approach? Yes, but you are all feeling the time squeeze. The pressure to make a decision is intense. Plus, there are other positions to fill, so taking someone – anyone – is better than no one. And it will save a tremendous amount of the team's time.

As you are probably thinking, this decision will undoubtedly come back to haunt you later, and you are more than likely right.

KEY POINT: *High-performing organizations spend the necessary time and effort to pick the right people. Experiencing short-term pain to create long-term gain is almost always worth it.*

Trusting Your Gut

"What a great interview! I really feel good about this guy! He was engaging – we had a great discussion. I just know he will fit into our culture and be a real asset to the team!"

I am amazed how many times I've heard this rationale come out of my own mouth. And the mouths of my colleagues and many others. Unless you have a good game plan and strategy, it is easy to get duped. I'm not suggesting that the candidate is legitimately trying to deceive you; they are just doing their best to try to land a job. I have learned through experience that some people are excellent in an interview. But what you initially see is not always what you end up getting.

I often suggest that good leaders learn to trust their instincts. But I say this in the context of business instincts. People are more complex. I have met only a small number who are good at reading people. When I say good, they are extraordinary, and in every case, they were trained professionals.

Developing and utilizing well-thought-out behavioral interview questions is one way to deal with this issue without being professionally trained to read people. It allows you to get down into the weeds. Determine how they think, what work they did, how they did it, and what outcomes occurred as a result.

> **KEY POINT:** *Do not trust your gut (instincts) when it comes to hiring people. It is too easy to let emotion rule the day. The facts are what matters.*

"She's a Great Friend – I Owe It to Her"

I was fortunate that the manager of my manager took a keen interest in me. He treated me like I was a good friend. His name was Larry, and during the time that I worked with him, he shared many of the lessons he had learned during his career with me. These came typically during impromptu discussions in his office when I was in town. He always tried to make time for me.

I enjoyed our discussions so much that I would try to get on his calendar for lunch whenever I came into the home office. I did this for more than ten years.

Guess how many times he went to lunch with me? Once! One lousy time in ten years! I couldn't understand why! It wasn't until many years later that I figured it out.

Larry taught me an important lesson by example. If he had gone with me every time I came to town, others would have taken notice. An assumption of favoritism would have begun to spread, which would have been bad for my career.

He kept the relationship professional. He was a friend, a trusted advisor, a colleague. He was never a buddy, a pal, or someone who would hang out with me on the weekends.

I also discovered that whenever we did meet, my boss was aware of it. Larry never gave me an assignment or did anything that would have jeopardized the relationship I had with my boss.

He managed the relationship so that no promotion expectation existed – based solely upon our relationship. The relationship was certainly an asset, but merit would rule the day. Because of this understanding, it never became weird or awkward. It was just as it should have been.

KEY POINT: *As essential as relationships are, promotions should be merit-based. It must be your ability to do the job well. Not because someone felt that they owed you a favor.*

Back to the workshop setting

If you remember, we put these managers of managers in groups of 4-6 and had them *make their confessions*. The items we just walked through are those that consistently show up on these lists most often.

After we talk through each one of the items on their lists, I typically say,

"We have discussed the *selection assumptions and mistakes* that you have made as a manager of managers. With your years of experience, you know they are mistakes. You know they are fraught with problems and issues. The question I have for you is this: Are you still making these same mistakes today?"

Their response is almost always, "Yes."

"What?" I ask in feigned surprise. "But you just said they don't work! Or, at best, you have a 50/50 shot of having a positive experience. Why would you take such a huge gamble?"

After a short pause, someone will typically say, "We don't have a better way of doing it."

Now, let me be clear, most organizations we work with have hiring processes and procedures. Some of them are detailed and thorough. They use personality profiles; they employ all kinds of tests and have teams of interviewers asking good questions.

But what we have observed is a general lack of clarity around the *management requirements*[c] and especially the *leadership expectations*[d] discussed with the candidate. Remember, some of the management requirements and many of the lead-

---

c   Chapter 2 – Management Requirements
d   Chapter 3 – Leadership Expectations

ership expectations are *unspoken and unwritten*. Therefore, the discussion often ends up defaulting back to their technical/functional competence. Why? Because most of the internal candidates interviewed for first-line manager promotions are individual contributors who have little or no management or leadership experience (in the way I have described it in this book).

If a hiring manager allows an interview to default to questions about their technical/functional prowess, it sends the wrong message to the candidate about expectations. The candidate may assume their technical/functional expertise is the priority.

Potential solution: Stay focused on the management requirements and the leadership expectations. Also, organizations must set up a system to ensure leadership capability is being developed at the individual contributor level long before someone is needed to fill a management position. Managers of managers should have the ability to observe the one vying for the management role *doing leadership-oriented work. They should also see them taking a Stage 3 approach to that work and ensure they enjoy it before promoting them!* Otherwise, they are rolling the dice.

But what if the company is *hiring from the outside*? How do they observe the candidate doing leadership-oriented work and taking a Stage 3 approach? Those responsible for interviewing should incorporate a strategy to ensure the candidate has transitioned to Stage 3. Otherwise, they can end up hiring a non-transitioned Stage 2 manager who has been wreaking havoc at the former company for the last five years. By utilizing well-constructed behavioral interview questions focused on the Stage 3 Key Accountabilities, a hiring team can flush out the *Stage 2 managers* and find the *Stage 3 managers*.

HOW TO USE THIS INFORMATION

For you, the reader, the one trying to decide if you want to follow the management track, the information you have received in this section: *Confessions of a Hiring Manager*, should be invaluable to you. It will tell you what to watch out for, so you don't end up the victim of a faulty assumption or common mistake of a hiring manager who is simply doing the best they can.

Recently, during one of our Leadership Transition workshops, one of the participants said, "I came into work one morning a few months ago, and my boss called me into his office."

"He pointed to a new organizational chart on the wall, and I was shocked to see my name on the chart as the new manager of my former peers. My boss was so pleased with himself! Like he had given me this wonderful gift – did me this huge favor.

"I was astonished! He had not even consulted me. He just did it. I'm still trying to decide if I want to remain in this position. It has been more than challenging for me," she concluded. Showing up to find out you have been promoted without being consulted is an unusual and unfortunate situation.

However, being pressured by a manager to move into a management role, *"Because I think you would be good at it,"* is not unusual at all. It is common.

Suppose you are currently being groomed for a position or being offered one. It would be in your best interest to ask yourself and those encouraging you to accept a management position some of the questions listed below.

Selecting a top technical/functional performer

- ◆ Am I considered one of the top technical/functional experts? Is this why I am receiving this offer?
- ◆ What other reasons do you feel qualify me for this position?

Time pressure

- ◆ Is there an urgency to fill this position? If yes, is that why you are considering me?
- ◆ If you had more time to search for the right candidate, would you still select me, or do you feel you could find someone more suitable?

Longest Tenure

- ◆ Have I been passed over on other promotions before? Do you (I) know why? If not, how can I find out?
- ◆ Am I one of the more senior or tenured candidates? Am I being considered for this reason alone? If not, what are the other reasons?

"We will lose her if we do not promote her"

- ◆ Have I ever threatened to leave if I didn't get my way?

Could there be a perception that I might quit if I don't receive a management position?
- If the answer to the previous questions is "yes," how can I remedy this situation? In what ways can I work with my manager to properly prepare for an opportunity?

"He reminds me of me"

- Do I have a good personal connection with any of the decision-makers?
- Do you/they think alike and agree on most issues?
- Am I being considered for the position for any of these reasons?

Settling

- Have there been any others interviewed for this position?
- Do I feel there are better candidates than me if they searched a little longer?

Trusting Your Gut

- Do I get the sense that they think I will be great at this without any evidence?
- Have I had the opportunity to manage or lead anything before? If yes, what were the outcomes?
- If not, what are some ways I could prove to you (and myself) that I have the capability?

"She's a Great Friend – I Owe It to Her"

- Are any of those involved in the decision my personal friends?
- If yes, do I sense this could play into the decision?
- Do I honestly feel I would be the best candidate?

Consider these questions carefully. Do not allow yourself to become an unwitting victim of a flawed decision. You should discuss any concerns with your manager or others who are part of the decision. Make sure you feel comfortable with the decision rather than doing something because you feel pressured. Every situation is unique. If you are at least aware of these issues, have asked the questions, thought through the answers, and still feel you should do it, then run with it!

There is nothing wrong with stepping into a management position if you are not 100% ready. You should not be afraid to push yourself, to stretch and grow. Just be self-aware and follow the recommendations found in this book. If you still feel good about the decision and feel you will get the support you need, then go for it – make it happen.

KEY POINT: *The ultimate responsibility for the decision to move into management must rest squarely on the shoulders of the one who will occupy the position!*

NOTE CONCERNING THE FINAL CHAPTERS

Having read the first six chapters of this book, you may have made your decision regarding management and feel there is no need to read the final two chapters: *Is Management for Me?* and *Choosing <u>Not</u> to Be a Manager*.

However, I highly recommend you <u>read both chapters</u> regardless of your decision, as they each have valuable information that will benefit you no matter which path you choose.

➤ CHAPTER SEVEN
IS MANAGEMENT FOR ME?

In the classic story, "*Alice's Adventures in Wonderland*," Alice happens upon the Chesire Cat, and she asks:

"Would you tell me, please, which way I ought to go from here?"

"That depends a good deal on where you want to get to," said the Cat.

"I don't much care where—" said Alice.

"Then it doesn't matter which way you go," said the Cat.

"--so long as I get somewhere," Alice added as an explanation.

John Tenniel. (1865). Alice and the Cheshire Cat.

"Oh, you're sure to do that," said the Cat, "if you only walk long enough."[32]

Too many professionals are like Alice – unsure of where to go, so they just keep walking, hoping, if they walk long enough, they will "get somewhere."

One reason for the uncertainty may be the lack of options for career advancement. Depending upon the organization, there may be a myriad of titles. But if you boil them down, most of them should fit into one of three broad categories:

- Individual contributor roles (e.g., software engineer).
- Informal leader roles (e.g., project manager – with no direct reports but has responsibility for a project, staffed with software engineers who each have a direct manager they report to).
- Formal manager roles (e.g., a supervisor who has direct line responsibility for people).

Unfortunately, there are a limited number of formal and informal opportunities, making it impossible for everyone to have upward mobility—if that's what they are after.

Therefore, career development options are either (1) stay in your current position or (2) try to get into a formal or informal management role—if you can find one.

REALITY CHECK

Fortunately, the *Stages of Impact Leadership Framework* (discussed in Chapter 4) provides additional options and improved ways to contribute and make an impact for those who can't find an opportunity or for those who do not want to manage. (More on this in the next chapter – Choosing <u>Not</u> to be a Manager).

That said, you may have already decided on the direction you want to head. However, I would encourage you to hang tight—wait to make that final decision. To apply a centuries-old expression that applies to this situation:

Measure Twice, Cut Once.

The meaning is obvious. Double-check before you make a decision or do something permanent. We refer to this as conducting a final *Reality Check*.

A Reality Check is:

"An occasion that causes you to consider the facts about a situation and not [just] your opinions, ideas, or beliefs."[33]

The process is simple, and it will provide you with the "*measure twice, cut once*" confidence you need to move forward.

KEY POINT: *Even if you have made a decision, doing a Reality Check will be eye-opening, and at a minimum, will identify areas where you may need specific help.*

THE REALITY CHECK PROCESS

Gather and review the answers to the questions at the end of each chapter. If you haven't completed them yet, now would be an excellent opportunity.

Chapter 1 – Begin With Your Motives (pp. 28-29)
Chapter 2 – Management Requirements (pp. 45-49)
Chapter 3 – Leadership Expectations (pp. 73-74)
Chapter 4 – A New Leadership Framework (pp. 112-113)
Chapter 5 – Management Blindspots (pp. 137-138)
Chapter 6 – Confessions of a Hiring Manager (pp. 159-162)

Review Feedback Assessment Data

- If you took advantage of the free online assessment in *Chapter 3 – Leadership Expectations*, gather it together now. If you did not but would like to do so now, you can access it here:
- Collect your assessment feedback. What do the ratings suggest? For example, are they consistently high or low? Are there specific items that you feel you should pay particular attention to?
- What do the comments in the "reasons why [you] would make an effective manager/leader of others" suggest?
- What do the comments in the "areas [you] should develop before accepting a management role" suggest?

WEIGH THE BALANCE

To weigh something in the balance means carefully studying it before deciding, looking at both the positive and negative repercussions or outcomes.

Review all your data. Consider what you feel are the positives and negatives.

Once you have gone through the *Reality Check* process, you should know where to go from here. Unlike Alice, you don't need directions from the Cheshire cat.

So what's it going to be?

Yes? No? Not now, maybe later?

You might struggle to decide at this point. If you do, my recommendation would be the last option: *Not now, maybe later.*

Whatever your choice, do not procrastinate! Be patient, but keep your feet moving—practice *active patience*,[e] be ready for an opportunity when it comes along.

> **Note:** Regardless of your decision, read the next chapter, "Choosing <u>Not</u> to Be a Manager," here is why:

- If you pursue management, you will eventually be leading people who are individual contributors faced with similar circumstances as those illustrated in Chapter 8. It would be powerful for you to understand their world as you work with them and attempt to provide guidance.
- If you are NOT going to pursue management, then *Chapter 8 – Choosing <u>Not</u> to Be a Manager* is clearly for you!

---

e   Chapter 3 – Leadership Expectations

➤ CHAPTER EIGHT
CHOOSING <u>NOT</u> TO BE A MANAGER

The focus of this book has been to help you decide if management is for you—but what if it isn't?

> **KEY POINT:** *If you don't want anything to do with managing people or projects, and you would prefer to stay in your current role as an individual contributor, then you should stay where you are!*

Those who beat the management and leadership drum should be careful not to play too loudly—lest they send the wrong message. Moving into management and leadership is not the only way to make a powerful impact.

You should not feel inferior in any way for <u>not</u> choosing to climb the corporate ladder. Every organization depends upon great people like you to help it succeed—individual contributors with specific technical or functional expertise, doing what they do best.

"TO BE, OR NOT TO BE: THAT IS THE QUESTION"

Arguably the most famous line from all of William Shakespeare's plays comes from his masterpiece, *The Tragedy of Hamlet, Prince of Denmark*.

In Act III, Scene 1, the main character, Hamlet, asks:

> *"To be, or not to be: that is the question."*

There is much more to Hamlet's statement (this is just the first line), and it has nothing to do with choosing not to be a manager.

However, we can adjust this question to make it meaningful and applicable to our topic. If you have decided not to be a manager, then you could alter the question in this way:

Lafayette - Photo - London. (1899). Sarah-Bernhardt (Hamlet).

> *"To transition or not to transition: that is the question."*

Here is what we mean by this: If you remain an individual

contributor, you can take one of two paths in the context of the Stages of Impact Framework from Chapter 4.

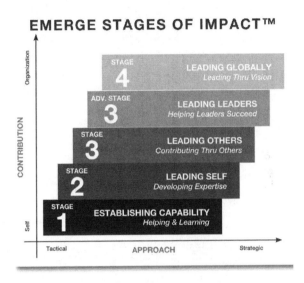

♦ Path One: Individual Contributor – No Transition

Selecting this path would encourage you to continue in your current role as an individual contributor focused on *Stage 2 – Leading Self*. Your approach will be *tactical*, and your contribution will be aimed directly at the expertise *you* deliver.

♦ Path Two: Individual Contributor – With a Transition

Selecting this path will allow you to continue in your current role as an individual contributor and, at the same time, work on making the transition to *Stage 3 – Leading Others*. Doing this will help your approach be more *strategic* and your contribution more focused on *others*. You will do this without the intention of moving into a management or leadership role where you are responsible for people or projects for now.

> **Note:** Team leader, project leader, supervisor, and manager roles can always be an option later if you change your mind.

Let's review both paths along with the advantages and disadvantages of each.

PATH ONE: INDIVIDUAL CONTRIBUTOR – NO TRANSITION

If the thought of making a transition to Stage 3 does not appeal to you, there is absolutely nothing wrong with this, and you should not feel pressured to do so.

If your objective is to simply come into work, focus on your technical or functional expertise and go home at the end of the day, then Path One is your best option.

Advantages

There are specific advantages to this path. For example, you will continue to enjoy a structured work environment, providing an opportunity to maintain a healthy work/life balance.

You can focus your efforts on becoming among the best in your profession.

> **KEY POINT:** *You must resist the temptation to be content with the status quo. Embrace all change that applies to your profession. Otherwise, you will become obsolete. Your value in Path One will be your ability to remain relevant.*

Disadvantages

The most significant disadvantage of Path One is related to your approach and contribution. At some point in your career (generally 8-10 years), others will begin to assume that you should be more strategic in your approach and more people-oriented in your contribution (Stage 3).

Be prepared for this to happen. It does not mean you have to meet those expectations, but they will be there and will influence how others view the impact and value you deliver to the team and organization.

Some who select Path One may prefer to work alone, losing themselves in their work and avoiding people as much as possible. In the future, work will likely become more collaborative, not less. Therefore, you may need to deal with people more than you do now to get your part of the project done. Technology will undoubtedly help but prepare for a possible increase in personal interaction with others.

Example of an Individual Contributor – No Transition

Tom was someone I admired greatly. He had been in his career a very long time, and by many standards, could have elected to coast out his remaining years, refusing to evolve and change to meet the expectations of his work environment. No one would have blamed him.

But Tom was not like that. He continued to embrace meaningful change, the type that would allow him and others around him to be more productive. He never retired but remained fully engaged and involved – every day doing the work he loved until he passed away in 2015.

A close friend of Tom's told us,

> "When Apple introduced the iPad in 2010, Tom saw the potential of it and wanted to be an early adopter. He began converting all of his work to that device. It took him some time and effort, but eventually, Tom was completely paperless. He was able to run everything through the iPad and his personal computer. Because he traveled a great deal, this allowed Tom to be highly productive while on the road."

This achievement may not seem all that remarkable, but Tom was born in 1922, making him almost 90 years old at the time. I find him inspiring. He did not fight change but embraced it, an excellent example of someone who followed Path One and remained relevant.

Scan code for more information on Leading Self - Path One.

PATH TWO: INDIVIDUAL CONTRIBUTOR – WITH A TRANSITION

If you are the type who wants to help grow the business and positively influence the people around you, but you do not want the added responsibility that comes with a management role, then this path is for you.

Advantages

The advantages of this path include not having to deal with several unpleasant interactions or activities that we expect managers to handle. Like disciplining team members for poor performance or being responsible for letting direct reports go.

Those who choose Path Two will not be responsible for delivering difficult news, navigating corporate politics, or participating in endless management meetings.

You will continue to enjoy a structured work environment and utilize your technical or functional expertise—with the added value that comes with a Stage 3 transition.

Making this transition will prepare you for the option of becoming a team leader, project manager, supervisor, or formal manager in the future if you decide later that you would like to pursue one of those positions. It will be much easier for you to make that move because you have transitioned.

KEY POINT: *Be prepared for what will happen as you transition. You will change. Your passion for <u>individual performance</u> will decrease, and your passion for <u>team performance</u> will increase. You will care more about the health of the business and the growth of your peers. The company and those you interact with will view you differently. You will become more valuable to them and more marketable both inside and outside the organization.*

Disadvantages

Because of your transition and mindset shift, you will not have the same passion for growing your expertise. You will still be able to develop it but not to the same degree. Why? Because you will likely be in higher demand. Managers and (or) project leaders will pursue you to join their projects because you see the business differently. The value that your approach and contribution bring to the table will be obvious.

A natural outcome will be increased demands on your time. You will need to be strategic in where you choose to spend your efforts.

Common Characteristics of a Transitioned (Stage 3) Individual Contributor

As you transition and experience this mindset shift, you will naturally approach your work more strategically; the contribution you make will be more others-focused. Characteristics that may become important to you and ultimately be a part of who you are, include:

- ◆ Help new employees get up to speed faster and more efficiently.
- ◆ Help coach and develop experienced employees in their work responsibilities.
- ◆ Use your networks of relationships (internal/external) to solve complex problems.
- ◆ Introduce others to your networks of relationships.
- ◆ Share your institutional knowledge and understanding of the organizational culture with others.
- ◆ Embrace and help drive positive changes in the organization.
- ◆ Help lead other individual contributors to higher levels of excellence.
- ◆ Lead the team when the boss is on vacation, in meetings, or otherwise unavailable.

Think about the impact you will have on members of your team and the organization by employing these approaches and the personal satisfaction you will enjoy at the same time!

> **KEY POINT:** *A Stage 3 individual contributor "can help a team be more engaged, [and] effective in solving problems. [They] build better brand recognition and service quality"ᶠ by positively influencing those who interact, communicate, and solve problems for our customers.*

> **KEY POINT:** *There is power being a peer versus a boss. The team sees the Stage 3 individual contributor as someone who understands their world and experiences the same challenges and obstacles. This connection increases trust and credibility, which leads to expanded influence— something badly needed in a highly competitive, rapidly changing marketplace.*

Example of an Individual Contributor with a Transition

About four years ago, I met Spencer. We ended up on the same team doing volunteer work for a non-profit service organization.

Spencer was in his mid-30s, soft-spoken but open and friendly. I could tell right away that he was a smart guy. He was observant, articulate, and had a sense of calm confidence.

f   Chapter 4 – A New Leadership Framework

One of our early conversations went something like this:

"What do you do for work?" I asked.

"I'm a cyber security analyst for a large pharmaceutical company."

"So, what does a cyber security analyst do exactly?"

"I am part of a group of highly specialized forensic computer experts that our company refers to as *Blue Team*. Our primary objective is to be proactive in detecting, defending, and strengthening our network from hackers who want to steal valuable information or cause other harm.

"We are constantly on the prowl for suspicious activity. We are hunters—stalking the individuals or groups responsible for the threat or potential attack. We use their tactics, techniques, and procedures against them as we look for evidence of a compromise."

"Fascinating!" I said. "That description makes me want to change careers! No wonder you love what you do."

Spencer looked pleased.

"What about you?" He asked. "What do you do?"

"I am co-founder of a leadership development company called Emerge Leadership Group. We focus on transitions."

"What do you mean by transitions?" He asked.

"Here is an example; let's say you know a cyber security analyst who receives a promotion to a position where he manages other cyber security analysts.

"The move, from being a doer to a leader, is a transition. This particular transition is challenging because of the dramatic change the person must undergo from taking care of oneself to having responsibility for an entire team. It's pretty demanding, and most people struggle. We have tools, assessments, and a learning process to help professionals navigate it successfully," I concluded.

"Really?" Spencer said.

"I have been thinking a lot about this very topic. My boss has been encouraging me to consider moving in the management direction. You'll have to give me some pointers," he said hopefully.

"Of course," I said.

"Coincidentally, we just completed an on-demand, self-paced version of our Leadership Transition training course for those making this very transition, which fits your situation perfectly," I said.

"I'll make you a deal. I will give you free access to it if you give me honest, constructive feedback on how we can improve the program."

"That would be great!" Spencer said, trying to contain his excitement.

He began working through it the next day.

When he finished, we reviewed what he had learned and what he needed to develop. I recommended he find an assignment or project to apply the concepts and ideas he generated during the course to grow his leadership capability. He identified one, met with his manager, and received approval. It was high-profile enough for others to see him in action and recognize his potential.

* * *

A few months later, following some evening meetings, Spencer said:

"My company offered me a management position."

"Really? And what did you tell them?" I asked.

"I told them I didn't feel that now was the right time.," he said confidently.

"Why not?" I asked, knowing that he would likely give them the answer he did.

"I want to continue to work on my technical skills. There is so much more I need to learn," Spencer said.

"I feel like I need some additional technical development time. I need to gain more credibility among my peers. Also, I would prefer to make the transition to Stage 3 first, then decide if I want to remain in my current position or pursue a management position."

* * *

Several months later, Spencer was offered a position with one of the world's most prominent and successful cybersecurity companies.

"My official title is *Senior Consultant*," Spencer said proudly.

"It's an individual contributor role, but a high-profile one! Working for this organization in this role will give me a huge credibility boost," he concluded.

As I discussed it with him, I learned that he wasn't looking for a job – the job came to him. Why? Because he was practicing *Active Patience*.[34] For example, Spencer found out who the influential people were in his industry – the players.

He then did some research and discovered what associations they belonged to and which conferences they attended.

He became involved and connected. He built relationships with people who mattered. Here was a guy who didn't go out of his way to make friends – it wasn't particularly natural for him. And yet, he pushed himself in uncomfortable ways.

Spencer was not pounding on their door, begging for a position. He was taking action, growing his technical ability while building reciprocal relationships—a Stage 3 Key Accountability.

When the position opened up, the choice was easy. There wasn't much of an interview process. The manager making the decision knew Spencer and his abilities. In his mind, Spencer was an obvious choice. I was impressed.

Spencer was applying what he had learned about making a transition to Stage 3 as a nonmanager.

"In addition to building relationships with others, what else have you discovered about yourself as you have worked on making this transition?" I asked.

Spencer reflected for a moment.

"I have learned that I like to help others be successful—more than I thought I would. If you had told me five years ago that I would eventually enjoy this, I would not have believed you."

"Another thing, I like process improvement, but I think about it differently now. My time perspective has changed. I feel like I'm looking at things on more of a long-term basis now, and I'm considering a much larger group of people and departments in the organization. When I used to think about process improvement – I focused only on my little island. Now it is much bigger."

"So, what are your next steps to keep the transition moving?" I asked.

"I am going to continue to attend meetups, working to make innovation happen. I will take the initiative, look for solutions, work with my peers, and do all of it without managing them. I still have some major things to work on, including my communication skills. When challenging subjects come up, I tend to be a little too direct, and it creates tension."

"My goal is to be a Stage 3 individual contributor," Spencer concluded.

"Spencer, I believe this is perfect for you right now. You're well on your way to becoming a Stage 3 leader regardless of the role or position you choose to take," I said confidently.

KEY POINT: *Advance your career by transitioning to Stage 3. Then make a horizontal move to a different part of the company to broaden your skill base, develop new relationships, and improve your leadership capability. The transition to Stage 3 is portable and will provide tremendous value to you wherever you might go in the future.*

➤ CONCLUSION

To conclude, let's jump back to the *Introduction* and, in the spirit of *"Begin with the End in Mind,"*[35] review the approach and objectives we started with:

> "This book takes a preemptive approach to the self-imposed question, 'Is Management for Me?' It also has a dual purpose:
> - If you decide management **IS** for you, *this book will significantly increase the probability of your success by helping you prepare for the role <u>before</u> stepping into it.*
> - If you decide management **IS NOT** for you, *this book will help increase the impact you can make to the organization as an individual contributor—in a profound way.*
>
> "So, whether you decide to pursue management or not, it will be a win for you!"
> *(Introduction – Why You Need to Read This Book)*

* * *

I sincerely hope we have made good on these commitments to you.

Those leaders who stand out, who make the most significant contribution, understand and meet the expectations illustrated in the *Stages of Impact Framework*.[36] The most important opportunity is on the frontline, where the largest leadership gap exists. Making the transition from Stage 2 to Stage 3 as a manager, supervisor, project manager, team leader, or individual contributor puts you in a position to seize this opportunity.

This transition will become even more critical as the pace of change continues to accelerate. You can fill the leadership gap – as a manager or a nonmanager.

Follow the process, move forward – make a difference!

THE EMERGE LEADERSHIP JOURNEY

Executive Leadership
- Executive Transition Workshop
- Executive Sponsorship Session
- Executive Coaching

EXECUTIVE LEADERSHIP

EXECUTIVE LEADERS

LEADERS OF LEADERS

Leaders of Leaders
- Maximizing Your Impact™ Workshop
- Coaching for Impact™ Workshop
- Individual and Team Coaching

STRATEGIC LEADERS

Experienced First-Line Leaders
- Advanced Skills Workshops
- Expanding Your Leadership Capability
- Coaching for Impact™ Workshop
- Individual and Team Coaching

EXPERIENCED FIRST-LINE LEADERS

SEASONED LEADERS

New First-Line Leaders
- QuickStart™ Workshop
- The Leadership Transition™ Workshop
- Core Leadership Skills Workshops
- Coaching for Impact™ Workshop
- Individual and Team Coaching

NEW FIRST-LINE LEADERS

TRANSITIONING LEADERS

INDIVIDUAL CONTRIBUTORS

Individual Contributors
- Influence Without Authority
- Is Management for Me?™

➤ ACKNOWLEDGEMENTS

Late one evening in May 2020, I received an unusual phone call from my business partner and co-founder of Emerge Leadership Group, Jim Wentworth, who lives outside of Boston, MA, USA.

We had been working together for nearly twenty years, and this was the first time he had *ever* called me this late (12:30 am his time). There was a sense of urgency in his voice, and I wondered if something tragic had happened.

He has never been one for "chit-chat," and that night was no exception. He said, "Sheldon, we have to write the book!"

"What book?" I asked.

"*Is Management for Me?*" he said, with more than a hint of excitement.

At that moment, I knew he was right.

Although this book is written primarily in the first person, I consider Jim in every way a co-author. These are concepts and ideas that we have worked on and refined together. Without his knowledge, expertise, and support, this book never would have come to be.

* * *

I feel a deep sense of appreciation to Theresa Wilson, Carol Delisi, Kristina Kress, Mark Pavich, Chad Angeli, Bill Schmid, Cindy Whitehead, Connie McKellar, Megan Loar, Heather Weekes, Heidi Robbins, Ryan Robbins, Holli Merrell, Trevor Merrell, Sherri Merkley, Spencer Drew, Mike Hatch, Lacey Fuller, Laura Scott, Michael Hurley and Brian Coon. Their donation of time in reading, editing, and providing suggestions and feedback was invaluable.

A thank you to John Craven, Sr., and Todd Runyan for their continuous prodding. For many years they encouraged me to write a book. They didn't specify what kind of book. They just felt that I should write one. Thanks for believing in me.

I pay special tribute to my wife, Sherry, and our son, Justin, for their particular interest in every aspect of the process, from the cover design and internal book design to the content details. They spent many hours helping revise and refine this work. Their efforts have been particularly helpful.

* * *

We owe a debt of gratitude to our friends and clients, Matthew Ellis & Jane Woytowich of the Federal Reserve Bank of Philadelphia; and Ethan Campbell & Annalese Larson of the Tennant Company, who offered to test-drive this content in the classroom. Their trust in us to try this new concept was essential to its creation.

* * *

The oft-quoted statement made by Isaac Newton in a letter to Robert Hooke in 1675, "*If I have seen further it is by standing on the shoulders of Giants,*"[37] is appropriate here as we reflect on our journey. The many years of research and development in the creation and evolution of the Emerge Stages of Impact Framework would have been much more arduous without the remarkable works of these *Giants* whom we recognize and acknowledge for their groundbreaking concepts and ideas:

a. Dalton, G.W., Thompson, P.H., & Price, R.L. (1977). *The Four Stages of Professional Careers – A New Look at Performance by Professionals.* Organizational Dynamics.

b. Charan, R., Drotter, S., & Noel, J. (2001). *The Leadership Pipeline. How to Build the Leadership Powered Company.* Jossey-Bass.

c. Drucker, P.F. (2006). *The Effective Executive. The Definitive Guide to Getting the Right Things Done.* HarperCollins.

➤ NOTES

INTRODUCTION: WHY YOU NEED TO READ THIS BOOK

1   Emerge Leadership Group. (2015). *The Leadership Transition. For Leaders of Others*. https://emergegroup.com/our-solutions/first-line-leaders/

2   Emerge Leadership Group. (2014). *Maximizing Your Impact. For Leaders of Leaders*. https://emergegroup.com/our-solutions/leaders-of-leaders/

3   Emerge Leadership Group survey data collection of more than 9,000 Human Resource, Talent Development, and Organizational Development leaders from 2008 – 2021.

4   Mcfeely, S. & Wigert, B. (2019, March 13). *This Fixable Problem Costs U.S. Businesses $1 Trillion*. Gallup. https://www.gallup.com/workplace/247391/fixable-problem-costs-businesses-trillion.aspx

CHAPTER 1: BEGIN WITH YOUR MOTIVES

5   Note: If you need proof that money alone does not sustain long term job satisfaction, just Google it, there is an enormous amount of supporting data.

6   Rogers, J. (2008, November 25). *Post-Tensioned Slabs*. Concrete Construction. https://www.concreteconstruction.net/how-to/construction/post-tensioned-slabs_o

7   Emerge Leadership Group. (2015). *The Leadership Transition. For Leaders of Others*. https://emergegroup.com/our-solutions/first-line-leaders/

8   Lab Pro. (2021, June 13). *"Beakers are commonly used as a vessel to dilute concentrated chemicals, make buffers, or catch products during an experiment. Cylindrical measuring containers used in experiments with various substances for scientific purposes."* https://labproinc.com/blogs/laboratory-equipment/beakers-vs-graduated-cylinders-the-pros-and-cons-of-common-lab-glassware

9   Johnston-Jones, J. (2020, October 12). https://www.drjenniferjones.com/parenting-resources/the-true-meaning-of-discipline

CHAPTER 3: LEADERSHIP EXPECTATION

10   Mohsin, M. (2020, April 3). *10 Google Search Statistics You Need to Know*. Oberlo. https://www.oberlo.com/blog/google-search-statistics

11   Mischel, W., Shoda, Y., & Rodriguez, M.I. (1989, May 26). *Delay of gratification in children*. National Library of Medicine. https://pubmed.ncbi.nlm.nih.gov/2658056/

12   Mischel, W., Shoda, Y., & Peake, P.K. (1988, April 5). *The nature of adolescent competencies predicted by preschool delay of gratification*. https://pubmed.ncbi.nlm.nih.gov/3367285/

13   Christensen, D.A.

14   Emerge Leadership Group. (2015). *The Leadership Transition. For Leaders of Others.* https://emergegroup.com/our-solutions/first-line-leaders/

15   Emerge Leadership Group. (2014). *Maximizing Your Impact. For Leaders of Leaders.* https://emergegroup.com/our-solutions/leaders-of-leaders/

16   Hoekstra, D. (2021, February 12).

17   Braude, J. (1964). *Braude's Treasury of Wit and Humor* (p. 175)

18   Beck, R.J. & Harter, J. (n.d.) *Why Great Managers Are So Rare.* Gallup. https://www.gallup.com/workplace/231593/why-great-managers-rare.aspx

CHAPTER 4: A NEW LEADERSHIP FRAMEWORK

19   Online Etymology Dictionary. (n.d.) *Hyperdrive (n.).* https://www.etymonline.com/search?q=hyperdrive

20   Dictionary.com. (n.d.) *Synergy.* https://www.dictionary.com/browse/synergy

21   PBS.com. A Science Odyssey: People and Discoveries. *Ford installs first moving assembly line.* (n.d.) https://www.pbs.org/wgbh/aso/databank/entries/dt13as.html

22   Linda Hill, in support of the changes that must occur in these three areas stated, "*It becomes clear that the transition to manager ... constitutes a profound transformation, as individuals learn to think, feel, and value as managers.*" Hill, L.A. (1992) *Becoming a Manager, How New Managers Master the Challenges of Leadership.* Harvard Business School Publishing.

23   Hoffman, M. (2002) *The Emperor's Club.* Universal Pictures. Film.

24   *Ibid.*

25   *Ibid.*

26   Vocabulary.com. (n.d.) *Approach.* https://www.vocabulary.com/dictionary/approach

27   Federal Aviation Administration. (2016, November 28). *Airplane Flying Handbook:* (FAA-H-8083-3B). *Approaches and Landings* (p. 1)

CHAPTER 5: MANAGEMENT BLINDSPOTS

29   Unkrich, L. & Stanton, A. (2003) *Finding Nemo*. Buena Vista Pictures. Film.

30   One of the Key Accountabilities of *Stage 3 – Leading Others* in the Stages of Impact Leadership Framework found in Chapter 4.

CHAPTER 6: CONFESSIONS OF A HIRING MANAGER

31   Emerge Leadership Group. (2014). *Maximizing Your Impact. For Leaders of Leaders.* https://emergegroup.com/our-solutions/leaders-of-leaders/

32   Carroll, L. (1865). *Alice's Adventures in Wonderland*, New York: Macmillan.

33   Cambridge Dictionary. (n.d.) *Reality Check.* https://dictionary.cambridge.org/us/dictionary/english/reality-check

CONCLUSION

35   Covey, S.R. (1989). *The 7 Habits of Highly Effective People, (Habit 2),* New York: Simon & Schuster

ACKNOWLEDGEMENTS

37   Bariso, J. (2019, December 29) *12 Brilliant Qoutes From the Genius Mind of Sir Isaac Newton Physicist.Mathematician. Inventor. Mechanic. Author. Philosopher. Genius.* Inc. https://www.inc.com/justin-bariso/12-brilliant-quotes-from-the-genius-mind-of-sir-isaac-newton.html

Made in the USA
Columbia, SC
02 April 2022